Ron DelBene
Mary & Herb Montgomery

Christmas
Remembered

Ron DelBene
Mary & Herb Montgomery

CHRISTMAS REMEMBERED

UPPER
ROOM BOOKS
NASHVILLE

Christmas Remembered

Cover Design by Jim Bateman
Cover Photograph by Fred Sieb
First Printing: August 1991 (10)
Library of Congress Catalog Number:
ISBN:0-8358-0650-2

Printed in The United States of America

To Charla Honea,

who planted the idea for this book,

and to all the people who so kindly shared

their Christmas remembrances

Also by the Authors

From the Heart

The Into the Light Collection:

Into the Light
When I'm Alone
Near Life's End
A Time to Mourn

The Times of Change, Times of Challenge Series:

When You Are Getting Married
When Your Child Is Baptized
When You Are Facing Surgery
When an Aging Loved One Needs Care

The Breath of Life Series:

The Breath of Life
Hunger of the Heart
Alone with God

Table of Contents

Introduction

The idea for this book came about when my coauthors and I were in Nashville meeting with editors from The Upper Room. The discussion centered on the power of storytelling and my book *From the Heart*. My mention of one of the stories included in the book prompted someone to laugh and say, "That reminds me of the time when. . ." and that reminded someone else of a story and on it went.

Our meeting took place close to the holiday season and someone suggested publishing a book in which people share their Christmas stories. Suddenly we were off again, laughing over our special remembrances, feeling the tenderness of one another's words, trying to contain our individual stories until others finished telling theirs. Because we were so eager to share our Christmas stories, we were sure that others would want to do the same. And so the idea for *Christmas Remembered* was born.

Then came the task of gathering stories, and what a pleasure that turned out to be. Some of the contributors wrote their stories. Others told them to us either in face-to-face conversations or in telephone interviews. When we asked people to recall their memorable holiday experiences, most did not take very long to collect their thoughts. The stories were ready to be told; all people needed was an invitation from someone who respected the importance the memories held for them. Gathering the stories was like being ushered into the private den or sunlit porch of people's minds and hearts.

The range of the remembrances included here reflects our diversity as well as the feelings and values that are part of our common humanity. Some of the stories are humorous;

others are nostalgic. Still others are poignant in that they speak of difficult experiences that still call forth sadness even after many years. Remembrances shared by some of our contributors reveal that their greatest satisfaction comes from reaching out to others. From one another's stories we learn what gives joy and what brings pain; what causes anger and what brings peace. The stories we gathered provide windows through which we look at the experiences that shape people's lives and discover that the best gifts often come wrapped in life's painful lessons.

Telling our Christmas stories seems especially appropriate in that the birth of Jesus is told in story form. The Christmas Story is the Good News of God's son coming to live among us. Through the life and teachings of Jesus, we discover wherein our treasure lies. Jesus did much of his teaching in parables—stories that to this day invite personal interpretation and application to our lives. How appropriate it is to celebrate the birth of a storyteller by sharing our own Christmas stories.

Ron DelBene

Our Friend Bill

In the early 1970s, my husband, two young children, and I moved to Eugene, Oregon. We had no relatives nearby and we missed our parents who lived back in the Midwest. There was a nursing home within walking distance of our home, and we decided to go there to see if any of the residents lacked for visitors. I think we were trying to assuage our loneliness as much as we were trying to meet the needs of the residents.

Someone on the nursing home staff gave us three names and we went to visit the first two, a man and a woman. The third name we were given was Bill Brown. We went into his room and introduced ourselves and our children, who were then two and four. "Hi there, kiddies," he said. "Let me show you something." Sitting down on the bed, he whipped off his sock. We all gasped at his unearthly purple foot that had three toes missing.

Bill assured us that he was not in great pain, and clearly he was having a wonderful time astonishing his visitors. He told us he had traveled from one end of the country to the other by boxcar. While traveling through Eugene, he caught his foot in the coupling between two cars and lost his toes. He would be in the nursing home until his foot healed.

Our family visited Bill several times and we all grew very fond of him. Then, just before Christmas, he announced he was going to visit his sister in Boston. We couldn't believe he planned to travel all the way across the country with nothing but the clothes on his back. When we asked how he planned to get through the cold winter country, he said he hadn't really thought about that; he just figured he would go by boxcar and somehow stay warm.

Finding suitable clothes for Bill became our family's little Christmas project that year. We went to every thrift store we could find and got him shirts and pants, a belt, and even a wallet and a hat. Friends who heard about our project also donated things. We didn't collect a lot, but finally we had all the basics except for a warm coat, which we absolutely could not find in Eugene. The climate there is quite mild and people didn't wear the kind of winter coat Bill needed.

On Christmas Eve we gift wrapped the wardrobe we had gathered, but we worried about the missing coat. Bill was going to leave a day or two after Christmas, and it looked as if we wouldn't be able to send him off in a coat that would keep him warm. Suddenly my husband said, "Just a minute, I'll be right back."

During those years we moved many times and often didn't unpack all our belongings; it was just too much work to keep unpacking boxes and packing them up again. I heard my husband banging and crashing in the garage where a lot of our things were stored. When he came back in the house he was carrying a coat over his arm. He had remembered that when we lived in the Midwest he had two winter coats—one a second best and the other a beautiful coat he had hardly worn. The coat he brought in from the garage was his best one. We put a big bow on it and then took all the clothes over to the nursing home.

Bill was never one to be at a loss for words, but that day he was speechless. We were thrilled, and Bill was thrilled, and it was probably the best Christmas we ever had.

Later the kids and I made a Christmas card for their dad. On it we put the quotation from Luke 3:11 that goes, "Whoever has two coats must share with anyone who has none." It was our way of saying how proud we were of him.

A few months later my husband became unemployed in Eugene and we moved back to the Midwest where he was hired by a company he had worked for previously. Then one day in January of the next year we got a call from the nursing home in Eugene asking if we were the people who had known Bill Brown. Such a horrible feeling came over me that I handed the phone to my husband.

Bill was dead. He had been found near a boxcar somewhere in Illinois. In his wallet was our address, which we had given to him in the hope that he might send us a postcard from here and there so we would know how he was. The people at the nursing home were trying to find a family member to claim his body and had tracked us down. We told them about the sister Bill was going to see in Boston. That was all we knew about him, because after we said our good-byes to Bill that Christmas of 1971, we never got a card or had any further contact with him. But we never forgot him, and I don't think he forgot us either. We were very touched that he had carried our address in his wallet. It seems we were the only friends he had.

Pat Hinton

How Caruso Came Into Our Lives

On our way to the Christmas Eve service at church, my sister and I were carrying cold cuts for a party afterward. As we walked along, I noticed a dog following us. He was just an ordinary mutt, light brown with a long snout and big ears. Gradually he edged closer and sniffed the bag of ham and corned beef. We kept chasing the mutt away and by the time we entered the church, he had disappeared.

However, that was not the last we saw of the mutt. As we knelt in prayer there he was again, sneaking in between us, his snout moving toward the bag of meat on the pew. My sister—champion of stray dogs and cats—looked around to see if anyone was watching. Seeing the parishioners joyfully imbued in the Christmas spirit and never suspecting a dog was under our pew, she surreptitiously tossed him a piece of ham. He gobbled it up and came back for more just when the choir broke into song. That's when the mutt joined the choir and howled.

All eyes were on us. My sister kept right on kneeling and covered her face with her hands as if deep in prayer. I shoved the bag of meat under my coat and stared straight ahead.

When the music stopped the dog was gone. But not for long! He was waiting for us outside the church, wagging his tail. I looked into his soulful eyes and walked on, but without much determination. I don't know whether it was the hypnotic look in the dog's eyes that got me, or his stray status that got my sister, but we made only halfhearted attempts to chase him away. He followed us all the way home and never left. As a tribute to his marvelous vocal rendition that Christmas Eve, we named the mutt Caruso.

Jean Robbins

A Present for Dad

My father worked in construction. Most winters there was no work, and sometimes even in the summer construction jobs were scarce. One year things were especially hard. We had no money for food so my father hocked his watch. It was a gold pocket watch that had belonged to his father, and I have the feeling that it belonged to his grandfather as well. This watch was very important to my dad and he didn't look right without it. When I picture him these many years later, he's taking the watch out and opening it to check the time. After he hocked it, he had to ask Mom the time or go to the kitchen and look at the clock on the wall.

When Christmas came that year Mother had managed to save a little money, although I don't know how. I suppose because she was very frugal and we lived simply. Anyway, there always seemed to be enough money to buy Christmas gifts for my little brother, Jeremy, and for me. But this year Mother had even saved enough to get Dad's watch out of hock. Jeremy and I went with her to get it. We were excited about giving it back to Dad for Christmas and talked about how happy he would be because he missed the watch so much.

Whenever my dad felt low because he wasn't providing for his family, he drank. This particular winter he hadn't had work for a long time, so his drinking increased. Around Christmas he was drinking a lot, and on Christmas Eve he didn't come home. And he didn't come home.

It was snowing heavily and we were all very worried. We tended not to talk to one another about Daddy. It would have been helpful if we had been able to, but we each kept our thoughts to ourselves and worried in silence.

17

Finally my mother got a call from the police. They told her that Daddy was in jail; he had been picked up for drunk driving. Mother was relieved that at least he was safe and she didn't have to worry about him anymore that night. He would be home the next day for Christmas, she said. I went to bed feeling very angry that he wasn't with us on Christmas Eve. Even though the watch was wrapped and under the tree, I had ambivalent feelings about giving it to him.

We lived in an old farmhouse situated on twenty acres of land about three miles from Independence, Missouri. The land belonged to my grandmother and we lived on it for minimal rent. Our place was far enough out in the country that we couldn't see houses on either side.

Christmas morning my brother and I stood looking out the window waiting for our father. But instead of seeing our car drive up the hill from the highway that ran in front of our house, we saw Dad walking toward us. I don't know why the police didn't let him drive the car home; I never got that part of the story. But there he was making fresh foot-prints in the new blanket of snow that covered the farm. I wanted in the worst way to say to my mother, "Let's not give him the watch. He doesn't deserve it." But much as I felt like speaking up, I didn't.

Dad came in the house and stomped the snow off his shoes. We were all cool toward him because he wasn't home when we got up and Mother said we couldn't open our gifts until he arrived. Dad sat down and acted like he knew things weren't right—kind of like a little kid with a sheepish look on his face. We opened our gifts then. There weren't a lot, but we took great pleasure in whatever we got.

Mother asked my brother to get the gift for Dad. Jeremy went to the tree, picked up the package, and handed it to Dad. We all watched as he opened it. When Dad saw the watch, tears filled his eyes, then ran down his cheeks. It was the first time I ever saw my dad cry. Picking the watch up, he held it gently in the palm of one hand while he ran the fingers of his other hand over it. He didn't have any words; he just sat there crying. I remember having a sudden grown-up insight that my mother did the right thing by giving Dad the watch. It was his. And he was our father. And he should have it. Finally he said, "Thank you," and that was that.

Anna O'Mara

Flight for My Life

Early in Advent, I drove my mother and son to the Birmingham Civic Center where we were going to a concert. As I dropped the two of them off in front of the concert hall and went to park the car, I anticipated a wonderful evening at the symphony. Because a rock concert and other activities were going on at the civic center that night, I had great difficulty finding parking.

I had driven about three long blocks into a deserted, semi-industrial area when I finally found a parking spot. I was about to take it when an inner voice said, *It's probably better to pull a U turn and head back toward the civic center and park on the opposite side of the street.* That's what I did because I have come to instinctively trust this inner voice. I parked behind a very large van and turned off the engine. Again my inner voice spoke: *You really are too close to that van. If the driver is in a rush to get out, your car could get banged.* I started the engine and backed up so the driver of the van had plenty of room to pull out.

I took the keys out of the ignition and was about to open the door when I noticed a white car stopped at the intersection about a hundred feet away. A man holding what appeared to be a paper bag with a bottle in it got out of the rear of the car. I made a move to get out of my car when I thought, *Maybe I should just wait until this car pulls away.* I wasn't feeling apprehensive, just prudent; I sat there waiting. When the man got back in the car, instead of driving away as I had anticipated, the driver backed up and parked his car behind mine. I assumed that they were going to the rock concert and realized this was as close as they would be able to park.

I proceeded to try to open the door, but since I wasn't driving the car I usually drive I fumbled in the dark for the door release. I couldn't find it and was becoming impatient with my ineptitude. I couldn't understand why I could not find it. Unbeknown to me, at that instant this delay was one in a series of things that may have saved my life. As I continued to grope, the white car that had been behind me pulled alongside. The passenger front door sprang open and suddenly, without warning, a man stood there with a short-barreled shotgun aimed at my head. "GET OUT OF THE CAR!" he screamed. "GET OUT OF THE CAR!" He tried to open the door, but "fortuitously" it was still locked.

As I looked into the man's eyes, I knew that I had met with total and absolute evil: the expression on his face, the tone of his voice, the look in his eyes—the evil was almost overwhelming. I realized that I was confronting the most dangerous situation I had ever faced. At that moment, God spoke to me through that inner voice and communicated not through words but a sense of knowing: *You can't get out of the car. You cannot obey his screaming order. You must resist by fleeing. It is better to die resisting than as a victim of evil. You must fight by fleeing.*

All of this was communicated to me in a one-second flash of knowing. I did not hesitate for an instant. I knew the voice was right. If I got out of the car, the consequences would be horrendous. I had to take my chances and try to get away. As I put the key in the ignition, I saw out of the corner of my eye that other men were getting out of the white car. Luckily my car started without hesitation. Because the white car was parked absolutely parallel to mine—and because I had backed my car up—I had enough space in front of me to turn out of the parking space and into the street. Without turning my headlights on, I drove as fast as I could, hoping the man would not pull the trigger. I drove in the direction of the civic center where there were two police cars. I reported what had happened and the police insisted that I return to the crime scene and make out a report.

Afterwards upon reflection I realized that given the choice of dying, trying to do something in the face of evil, or acquiescing to it by being a passive victim, I had chosen to act by trying to escape. I did everything in that situation in a couple of seconds. That's probably what saved me. It wasn't even that the words were going though my mind. It was much faster than that. It was a total communication.

God appeared to Moses in a burning bush and spoke to him. God doesn't have to manifest the divine power in such tangible ways. I believe that when we really listen, God sends us messages every day. We never know when we are going to encounter evil and have to deal with it. We need to listen to God in our lives so that we have God's strength. I have no doubt that God was there with me all of the time. I need only to talk to God and listen.

Because this happened during the Advent season, I reflected upon the experience in relation to Christmas. Evil and violence are such strong forces in the world. Christmas for me is the rebirth of love and each day a positive "can do" attitude has to be reborn within if we are to have the strength and power to fight against the evil that surrounds us.

What started as an ordinary December evening led me to one of the most frightening moments of my life. In that experience I "lived" the deepest meaning of the words of the Twenty-third Psalm. "The Lord is my shepherd. I shall not want. . . . Even though I walk through the valley of the shadow of death, I fear no evil; for thou art with me. . ." (RSV).

Barbara Kip

A Slammed Door

Christmas of 1987 was four days away, and I had been too busy to do any shopping for gifts or decorating of the house. So I wasn't in the Christmas spirit—not, that is, until I went caroling with a church group in San Francisco.

Up one street.

Down another.

At house after house people came to their doors and listened to our caroling voices. Many seemed surprised by our visit and brought out cookies for us. But at one house that had several steps up to the entrance we got a reception I'll never forget. After only our first verse of "O Come, All Ye Faithful," a man slammed his door shut.

Some of us were stunned into silence, and I was ready to walk sheepishly away. One of the carolers was not so easily discouraged and urged us to keep on singing. We were about to sing, "Yea, Lord, we greet thee," when the door that had been slammed opened again. Instantly, I prepared myself for what I expected to be a loud outburst like "Get out of here!"

There was no outburst when the man, a woman, and a child appeared in the doorway. The woman had a camera and snapped pictures of our little group of carolers huddled at the bottom of the steps. Then they thanked us for coming to sing to them. As we walked away, I found myself with my first Christmas gift of the season: the knowledge that we never know what a slammed door can mean.

Barbara Dumke

23

The Candle

I cannot show you the Christmas memento that means the most to me. It is long gone. The only thing that remains is the shared memory of a red, holly-berry candle that sat on our polished wood coffee table Christmas after Christmas when my brother, John, and I were children. My mother received the candle in a Christmas gift exchange. As soon as she brought it home, its full fragrance began making its way into our "meaning of Christmas."

It was a well-milled candle, standing perhaps ten inches high, with a deep red translucence. On its side was a carved star, sprinkled lightly with green glitter. It was a pleasure to hold the weighty, smooth cylinder and even more delightful to press it to our nostrils, inhaling the mysterious aroma.

We cradled the candle, smelled it, shared it, argued over it, and hid it from each other. There was something about the candle that we wanted both to possess and to preserve. We lit it sparingly because we wanted it to last, protecting it like parents of an only child.

And the candle did last for many years. Each Christmas at decorating time, John and I raced to get it, trying to be the first to unwrap its scented secret. Whoever reached it first raised the trophy triumphantly. Leaving the other decorations untouched, we studied it with new pleasure until we were satiated and our homage to the candle was done. It was a Christmas truth: the holidays could not begin for us until the sight and scent of the candle opened some childlike gateway.

Between Christmases, we kept the candle in a buffet cabinet in our dining room, wrapped in tissue paper that was softened and torn with the years. The candle maintained its haunting aroma, and perfumed the inside of the cabinet even more than if it had been made of sandalwood or cedar. Many times, in the heat of midsummer, we would open the lower door to get napkins or silverware for special occasions, and the scent wafted to us. We would grab the candle greedily and hold it to our noses, inhaling memories.

We probably had the candle for ten years. For children, we had been uncharacteristically frugal with it, metering out the amount of time that the candle remained lit, safeguarding our memories of other Christmases, but still enjoying them.

When finally I was a teenager, I got reckless with my Christmas memories. The candle became expendable. Alone in my room one Christmas, I burned it down, finished it off all at once, without my brother's knowledge. When he discovered the red puddle, he howled in anger and pain. Our unspoken rule of conserving the candle had been violated. The mystery and excitement of childhood Christmases, the camaraderie, the sharing—all of it—were gone in a thoughtless gesture.

It must now be twenty-five years since we last lit the candle. Yet I know that the memory of that crimson light is as deeply sealed in the lore of my brother's Christmases as it is in mine. Someday, I'll ask him about his thoughts on red candles. Someday, I'll find a holly-berry candle and send it to him.

Kristine Barta Heim

Author's Note: After I wrote this story, I decided I wanted to share the candle-memory with my brother. I went to a department store to buy a red holly-berry candle. There I was, alone, looking at candles, when a clerk passed through on his way to a break. He smiled as he saw me weigh three or four candles in my hand, then hold them directly to my nose and inhale. Twenty minutes later, I heard laughter and looked up. The same clerk, now off his break, was passing again. And I was still there, weighing and sniffing candles.

The Family Gift

When I was growing up, we lived on a farm in the sandy hill country of central Colorado. Denver was 160 miles away, and our infrequent trips there were always adventures. But the trip just before Christmas in 1947 promised to be the biggest adventure of all.

Our parents had told us we were going to have a different kind of Christmas that year. Instead of giving my brothers and me individual gifts as they had always done, my parents were getting one gift for the family. The gift was to be a new car, and we were going to Denver to buy it.

My brothers and I were elated. The fact that we weren't getting any other presents didn't really matter. The prospect of having our first brand-new car was excitement enough for one Christmas. What made things even more exciting was that we would be spending the night in a hotel—something my brothers and I had never done.

The Saturday before Christmas we went to Denver as planned and spent the day shopping for our new car. Everyone happily approved of the olive green 1947 Plymouth we ended up buying. Then it was on to the hotel where we checked into a room on the sixth floor. Considering that we were used to small farm towns with single-story buildings, this was really life in the big city.

About two o'clock in the morning, we were startled awake by the unfamiliar wail of sirens. The sound came closer and closer and then stopped right outside our hotel. By this time we were all at the window looking at the scene below. A man who had been struck by a hit-and-run driver lay in the street. The police were there with the lights flashing atop their cars. Medical people jumped out of the ambulance and tended to the victim. Then they placed him in the ambulance and drove off with the siren wailing. Accustomed as we were to quiet country life, we were all astonished by what had happened.

The next morning we left Denver and headed home in our car that carried the smell of newness. A few days later we drove it to church for the annual Christmas Eve program. When we got back home, we gathered around the tree in the living room. There were the usual mixed nuts Dad had gotten for us as well as the hard candy and fresh fruit that were a part of every Christmas.

My brothers and I understood that the car was our gift that year, so we weren't expecting anything else. But to our surprise, there was a present for each of us under the tree. I don't recall what my brothers got, but I remember my gift well. It was a black patent leather purse, and when I opened it, I found a pair of white dress gloves tucked inside.

All in all it was a memorable Christmas.

Viola Strobel Schroeder

That Wondrous Airplane

My mother was a social worker for many years and her specialty was working with unwed mothers. Sometimes she got calls from upper middle class parents who didn't want to be seen going to the welfare office but who needed advice and counsel about their daughters. Although these parents frequently offered to pay for her services, my mother would not take their money. However, she did find a way for them to contribute to her own Christmas gift-distribution program.

Over time my mother helped a lot of these grateful parents, and whenever they wanted to know what they could do for her, she said, "Well, if you have any good used clean clothes or toys, I'll take them." So it was that boxes mysteriously appeared in our garage. At Christmastime my mother sorted through the contents to determine what was suitable for this person or that. Then she drove around the countryside delivering gifts to her clients.

The Christmas I was nine years old, I passed through the garage one day and noticed the most wondrous airplane. It was made of metal and very big—about three feet long with a three-foot wingspan. Because we lived in Little Falls, Minnesota, the boyhood home of Charles Lindbergh, airplanes were of particular interest to me. Also, World War II was coming to an end and I was intrigued by anything that had to do with aviation. So the plane in the garage just *couldn't* be going out to the poor kids. Surely my mother would give that treasure to me. But as Christmas drew near, I got the news that it was being given to someone else. This seemed like the meanest thing a kid's mother could do.

Christmas came and went and the airplane disappeared. I suppose I kept reminding my mother how much I had wanted it by pouting as a kid might. In the spring she asked me to go along on a visit to one of her rural clients. My sisters and I took turns going on these trips. It was our mother's way of having private time with each of us and also of letting us see another side of life. Although she was raising three kids on a meager salary, she wanted us to know that there were people much worse off than we were.

We pulled up in front of an old farm house where a family with thirteen kids lived. The land was so hardscrabble that weeds would hardly grow on it. While my mother visited with the folks, I wandered about on my own. As I turned the corner of a weathered barn, I stopped short. Lo and behold, there was my airplane! A little boy, who was probably six, was pushing it through the sand and the grass and the dirt. In the time since I first spotted the plane in our garage, some maturity must have taken place because I was okay about this boy having it. The plane was about as big as he was, and he was having a whee of a time.

On our drive back to town, my mother never mentioned the plane. Yet I knew that she knew that I knew where the plane ended up. Many years later I found out that one of the boys in that family became a 747 pilot and another was a military flight instructor. I like to think that maybe receiving that airplane as a Christmas gift was a factor in determining what they did with their lives.

As for me, not getting that airplane didn't discourage my interest in aviation. At age thirteen I took my first flying lesson in a J-3 Cub. Even though I didn't go on to make a career of aviation, flying has always been an important part of my business ventures. But when I look back at the incident with the airplane, I realize that flying was the farthest thing from my mother's mind. She just wanted to teach me a lesson about life.

John Uldrich

Breaking with Tradition

My mother is a classic case of "shop-'til-you-drop." At Christmas, she inundates the family with gifts, for the most part buying clothes and items that catch *her* fancy. I'm sure she means well, but she rarely takes into account what people want. As a child I learned that if I asked for something, it was just about guaranteed that I wouldn't get it.

When my sister and I were kids, there were so many packages in our living room that we piled them up and crawled through the tunnels we created. The opening of gifts began about six o'clock on Christmas Eve and lasted until one or two in the morning. Everyone in the family exchanged presents with everyone else—this included aunts, uncles, and cousins. Although these relatives never spent Christmas Eve with us, they always sent their gifts beforehand. This helped build the mountain of packages to be opened before Santa arrived the next morning, when there would be still more.

After I married, the old traditions continued, and my husband and I exchanged gifts with all the relatives. But the year we both changed careers, we had no money for the usual crystal and silver. We were desperate for something to give. That's when I hit on the idea of giving photos I'd taken at the Fourth of July celebration and other family get-togethers throughout the year. From among my many shots, I selected a photo that seemed right for each person. I then had them blown up and mounted the prints in simple frames. That year marked our break with some old traditions and the start of new ones.

My husband, two children, and I still go to my parents' house to open presents on Christmas Eve. And we still exchange gifts with all the relatives, only now we think of things that are less commercial and more personal. Around Thanksgiving, we buy white narcissus bulbs which my six-year-old son and nine-year-old daughter like to help plant and then watch grow. By Christmas the plants are usually in bloom and ready to give as gifts.

As a child, I was never allowed to help with the decorating. Now that I'm a parent, I involve my children in getting the house ready for the holidays. I give them stencils and spray snow and they decorate the mirrors and windows in the upstairs bedroom. It makes a mess, but they are always happy with their handiwork. And so am I.

We also make ice candles by filling ice cream buckets with water and putting them in the freezer. When the water is frozen, we take the buckets out and chip a hole in the center of the ice. Then we take the ice out of the bucket and place a candle in the hole. We make about two dozen of these ice candle luminaries and line our driveway with them.

Each year we plan an outing to the Christmas show at a nearby children's theater or go to some other holiday performance. And, unlike my own family, we attend a church service on Christmas morning. Breaking with some of the old traditions and adding new ones has helped bring meaning and even a sense of joy to the celebration of Christmas.

Georgina Sand

A Moment of Grace

In 1986 I went to Namibia on the southwest coast of Africa to share in a clergy conference and visit parishes. When I returned to my home in Alabama, the only way I could describe my experience was to say that it was *inspirationally disorienting.* It was a feeling I continued to have until Christmas Eve almost a year later.

While in Namibia I was inspired by the faith of a people who believe that God is with us and that God saves. It was particularly inspiring to see that they held to their belief within a complex environment of apartheid and military brutality. But it was disorienting to think of two priests serving a parish with twenty thousand parishioners spread over nineteen outstations covering some forty kilometers with only a bike and a small pickup for transportation.

One blistering hot Sunday I stood in a cement-block, tin-roofed church where two hundred people sat on low benches of logs placed on the dirt floor. The priest, who wore nineteenth-century-style vestments, had to translate the liturgy into the people's dialect because there was not yet a prayerbook in their language. It was both disorienting and disconcerting to think that back home such small matters as new prayerbooks and hymnals provoked major arguments.

For a long time after returning from Namibia, I felt spiritually confused. I couldn't seem to put my experiences into focus and use them as a backdrop for God's action in my own life. Then at a midnight Christmas Eve Eucharist, which I attended with my family, things came together for me.

In the pew ahead of us that Christmas Eve sat a foster parent from the parish. With Mary was Suzanne, her new foster baby. Just before the beginning of the Christmas gospel, I asked Mary if I could hold the tiny infant and she said yes. There in my arms lay a mixed-race child born outside a family and given up for adoption at birth. After I held the baby for a time, I had the sense it was no longer just Suzanne I was holding. A flash of grace showed me that this fragile earth with all its inhabitants was cradled in my arms. We are all sisters and brothers, and because I have chosen to be a person of prayer, I was spiritually united with Suzanne as surely as I was with those gentle believers in Namibia. The understanding that through prayer I can embrace and enfold our planet and all its people was my most cherished gift that Christmas.

Ron DelBene

The Best Christmas Ever

The year I was thirteen, my father wasn't home to spend Christmas with my mother, brothers, sister, and me. He was suffering from depression and was a patient at Pilgrim State Mental Hospital. Because of the circumstances, Christmas for our family was very different from those in years past.

For me the holidays were the best time of the year. We always had a tree with presents under it. One Christmas I got both a portable radio *and* a record player. This seemed like such largess because we were not a wealthy family. But then nobody in our Brooklyn neighborhood was wealthy, so as children we weren't much aware of what we didn't have.

I can't recall if we had a tree the year my dad was ill or if there were gifts; I just remember that we spent the day at the state hospital. At the time we didn't have a car, so we went with relatives. Seeing my dad behind a door with bars was both startling and terribly sad. He'd had shock treatments and some of his memory was gone.

After our family's visit we passed through the hospital lobby where there was a large Christmas tree. I don't recall any other decorations; everything was very stark. Yet as I walked out the door toward the car I remember thinking, *This is the best Christmas I ever had.* Even as the thought came to me I was mystified. It had been a sparse Christmas and a season filled with anxiety about my father. But on some level I must have understood that Christmas is made special by being with the people you love. Even though our family was in a difficult situation, we had been together.

My father was hospitalized for six months. To support us while he was away, my mother worked in a factory. Her meager salary didn't cover our needs, so the church gave us food for Christmas, as they had for Thanksgiving. The head of the church charity was my best friend's father. Although it was awkward having him bring us food and receiving the small checks that we then took to the grocery store, I will always have enormous feeling for the goodness of the church.

My father was able to return to work after he was released from the hospital. Aside from one relapse that required medication, he lived many productive years and our family got on with life.

I married and had three children of my own. A few years into marriage, I began to feel a restlessness around the holidays that I couldn't explain even to myself. "Why don't we do something *different* this year?" I said to my husband. "Instead of spending so much time and money shopping, let's put our resources into something else. . . maybe meet a need someone has." Even though my husband didn't pick up on the suggestion, I kept making it year after year.

As the children grew older, I suggested to them that we reach out and try to brighten someone's Christmas. We have good kids—thoughtful and compassionate—but they didn't pick up on my suggestion either.

One day I was telling a co-worker about my desire to make Christmas less commercial and more a time for our family to give of ourselves. All of a sudden I realized why my husband and children were more satisfied than I was with Christmas the way we always celebrated it. They had not had my experience; their father had not been ill and away from home during the holidays. In that severe setting at Pilgrim State Hospital, I discovered that the really important thing about Christmas is people, and that reaching out to them in love and caring warms the heart and nourishes the spirit. When that happens, Christmas is the best it can be.

Rose Zuzworsky

The Year the Santa Myth Died

When I was six, our family traveled from Michigan to Florida to spend Christmas with Grandma Caird and Aunt Maureen. Florida wasn't as sunny or as warm as we'd expected. Rain had turned Grandma's front yard into a swamp, and there was no place to play.

One afternoon my father suggested that we go to Daytona Beach. "When you get home, you can tell everyone you went to the beach in December," he said. The weather remained damp and gray and the ocean was shades of brown, nothing like the photos in which the sky was always baby blue and the ocean aquamarine. Up and down the shore, families like ours scoured the sand looking for shells to take home as souvenirs. We found a spot where we could drive our '52 Chevy onto the beach, just like the drivers who raced in the Daytona 500.

On the boardwalk my father noticed a small building with a sign that read "Santa's Cabana."

"Marj hasn't seen Santa yet this year," my mother said. As the youngest in the family, I was my parents' only hope for someone still believing in Santa Claus. I was a first grader, though, and had grown skeptical.

I wanted to believe. Until the year before, I had truly believed. But logic and the doubts of other children wore down the magic, and I began to discover some practical flaws in the Santa story. Now, seeing him so out of place on Daytona Beach, I was hit with the truth: There was no Santa Claus.

If I didn't believe, though, would it ruin Christmas? Would I get any presents? Maybe my brothers and sister had gotten presents last year only because *I* still believed in Santa.

Warily, I stepped through the open door into Santa's Cabana, a tiny, roughsided shack with a fresh coat of paint. Inside was one wooden chair, where a tired-looking man in a Santa suit waited.

"Hello! What's your name?" he asked. If he was really Santa, he'd know who I am, I thought.

"Marjorie," I muttered.

"Marjorie! Well come sit on my lap."

"No."

Santa's red clothes were musty smelling and faded. His beard and white hair were matted. His black patent leather belt and boots were cracked and scuffed, like my shiny, new Easter shoes looked by the end of summer.

"You won't sit on Santa's lap?" He leaned forward and put an arm around my shoulders to pull me closer. "Why don't you just stand next to Santa then and tell him what you want for Christmas?"

If he was the real Santa, he'd know what I want, I thought. I'd written him a letter before we left for Florida, when I was still in the skeptical phase.

"My sister wants a parakeet."

"Okay, but what about you? What do you want?"

I wanted to leave. My parents were watching, though, and they seemed so excited about seeing Santa on the beach.

"I want a sweater set," I said. All the teenagers that year were wearing a short-sleeved pullover sweater with matching cardigan. As I'd written in my letter, I didn't want or need any toys.

"Anything else?" Santa asked.

If this was really Santa, I thought, he'd make sure he knew what color sweater set I wanted.

"Nope. That's it."

He reached into his brown paper bag and handed me a candy cane. "Merry Christmas."

"How about that?" my mother gushed. "Santa Claus in Florida!"

I couldn't believe my parents were still pushing the Santa story. Wasn't it the same as lying? They seemed to want me to believe. I felt I'd disappoint them if I said I knew there was no Santa.

I gave the candy cane to my sister. "I told him you want a parakeet."

That evening our Aunt Maureen took us to see the movie "White Christmas." As I settled into my seat with a box of buttered popcorn, I turned to my sister and whispered, "I know there's no Santa Claus."

On Christmas morning a parakeet chirped and chattered in a cage labeled "To Virginia from Santa." My present from Santa was a pink sweater set. It was the color I wanted and even more beautiful than I'd imagined. Tiny white pearls outlined flower designs on the cardigan. The box it was wrapped in, though, was marked "Dancer's Department Store," the store back home where my mother bought her knitting yarn.

Marjorie Barton

Angels in the Snow

One Saturday evening during the holiday season, my friends Ruth and Blue invited me to dinner at their home. It was an evening of good food, good company, and good conversation. There was serious talk about world affairs as well as laughter and the intimate talk close friends engage in. While we were having this warm, comfortable time inside, a fierce snowstorm howled outside. Conditions got so bad that Ruth and Blue insisted I spend the night.

By morning the storm was over; everywhere the snow lay deep and soft and dazzling. Blue began the job of digging out, and I got a shovel to help him. He was a life-loving teddy bear kind of guy, and after we got the walk cleared, we became kids again as we fell flat on our backs into a drift. Then, brushing arcs in the snow with our arms and legs, we made perfect snow angels.

That holiday season never seemed to lack parties, and the next weekend there was one to which Ruth, Blue, and I were invited. Ruth was supposed to help with preparations, but even when the party was well underway she still hadn't arrived. Someone called her at home and caught her just as she was returning from the hospital. Blue had suffered a massive heart attack and died.

I immediately left the party and headed for Ruth's house. On the way, I thought about Blue. For most of his working life he'd held high-level government jobs in which he worked hard for social justice. An admitted workaholic, he became demoralized when he lost his job a couple years earlier. But then he became enthusiastic about acupuncture and what it could do to improve people's lives. He went on to become a certified acupuncturist and opened his own clinic.

Although he still worked far too many hours, he was back to taking a broader delight in the world of people and things. He'd had previous heart attacks and been warned to lose weight and slow down. For the most part, the warnings went unheeded, and now he was dead at fifty-five.

That evening as I went to comfort Ruth, the air was crisp and the sky so clear that the stars shone with a particular brilliance. On my way up the front walk, I noticed the snow angels that Blue and I had made the week before. They were still in perfect form and the snow around them lay undisturbed. At that moment I felt a warm and reassuring connectedness with my friend. There are mysteries about life and death that we can never fathom, but I had a kind of knowing that Blue was in a place of peace and happiness far greater than anything we know on this earth.

Kate Kane

Christmas in the Land
Of the Morning Calm

Christmas of 1954 I was a young marine lieutenant serving in Korea. My wife and baby daughter—born since I left home—were back in the States. Instead of spending our first Christmas together with my new family, I was with a battalion of the 5th Marines, thirty miles north of Seoul.

Because of the general absence of wind in early morning, Korea is known as the Land of the Morning Calm. On Christmas morning, the description seemed especially apt. The thermometer hovered around zero and several inches of snow covered the ground. The sky was overcast, the air still. In the village across the frozen rice paddy, smoke rose in parallel columns from the thatched roof huts, continuing straight up until it dissipated. Smoke rose from our tent stoves, Quonset huts, and mess tents as well, but the smoke from kerosene was not so noticeable.

Both Protestant and Catholic chaplains scheduled services for Christmas morning. The services were to be held on the hillside near the mess tents and our battalion headquarters. This was the best place because our tents and Quonset huts were too small, besides being set up for other activities.

No one was required to attend services. I went out of respect for the chaplains, and to set a good example for the even younger marines. Nearly two hundred of us turned out for each service. We sat on our helmets in the snow. The dull gray-green of our uniforms and jackets was broken here and there by flashes of color from non-regulation scarves, mittens, sweaters, and knit caps. We faced a small portable altar and an equally small pump organ. The chaplains had no microphones, and the organ suffered from the cold. But both had enough volume to lead us in the hymns and prayers.

Our voices were as clear as the cold air. During the services with my fellow marines, I thought of all that was precious to me: home, my wife, my unseen infant child. I realized that Christmas does not depend on church architecture or fine clothing, expansive meals or expensive gifts. Christmas is best celebrated as a voluntary act in which we replenish our personal faith in the company of others. Overseas that year, in the Land of the Morning Calm, I realized that Christmas Day—in itself—is not important, but the faith it represents is.

Rex Pickett

Making Dreams Come True

---

*The year my daughter, Ann, was ten she wanted a doll for Christ-*mas. Not just any doll mind you, but one called Baby Precious. The children's TV programs that year were saturated with ads for Baby Precious; it seemed that no little girl's life would be complete without this doll to cuddle and call her own. But wise consumer that I considered myself to be, I was not going to be manipulated by advertisers. After all, Ann already had an entire shelf filled with dolls she rarely played with. And anyway, wasn't ten a bit old for dolls? So, with motherly wisdom, I decided that instead of Baby Precious, we would get Ann ice skates for Christmas.

It was our family custom to put all of the children's wrapped packages under the tree well in advance of Christmas. Much of the holiday excitement and fun came from holding, shaking, and trying to guess what was in each package. The size of the skate box suggested a doll. So did the weight and the way something thumped when the box was shaken. Ann was so sure she was going to find Baby Precious inside that she never even guessed at other possibilities. How wonderful, I thought, to have hit upon a gift that would really surprise her. And of course the gift would delight her as well.

At our house we open gifts on Christmas Eve. Long before it was time to begin, each of the three children arranged their presents in the order they were to be opened. The box believed to contain the most hoped-for gift was always first. There was no question about which gift was first for Ann. We all looked on as she tore away the wrapping and eagerly lifted the lid. But instead of the glee I had expected, I saw her smile slip away and her slender shoulders sag. She

44

had too much dignity to cry, but clearly she was crushed. I tried to brighten the moment by telling her how much fun we would have skating on a nearby rink and that she could take lessons if she wanted. Yet even as I spoke I knew that when the desire of your heart goes unfulfilled, words are no help at all.

During Christmas vacation, the children and I traditionally spent a few days with my mother. Even though she sent gifts that we opened on Christmas Eve, she always had an after-Christmas gift waiting at her house for each grandchild. My mother never consulted me about what they had already received or what they needed or wanted. These were simply extra gifts she selected because she thought they were right.

When Ann opened her grandmother's gift, I stared in disbelief, then in wonderment. Lying in a nest of white tissue paper, was Baby Precious—a sweet-faced doll wearing a yellow, puff-sleeve dress and white pinafore. On the pocket of the pinafore was a tiny embroidered bouquet of blue flowers. I watched Ann lift the doll from its box and saw the awed look on her face turn to one of total joy. At that moment I knew with certainty that Christmas is not a time for giving children what you think they should have, but a time for making dreams come true.

Mary Montgomery

In an English Tradition

---

*At seventy I have many Christmases to remember. As a child I re-*member Christmas Eve as being the greatest time of the year. That day we decorated our tree, which was usually a holly tree if one was available in the woods nearby. Though my father, an Englishman, was dead, we continued celebrating in an English tradition. We decorated our tree with red and white strings of cranberries and popcorn. A few ornaments were added to our collection over the years. Candle holders clipped on the branches of the tree held real candles.

On Christmas Eve we rode the street car to church for the midnight service. This was exciting to me, especially because we could stay up late, and after services we rode home in a taxi. Upon arriving home, we were forbidden to look in the parlor where the tree and presents were displayed. However, we did get to sit by the fire and drink a cup of tea before going to bed. The anticipation was wonderful.

The first thing Christmas morning we lighted the candles on our tree for a few minutes, all the while watching them carefully. Then we opened our gifts. One year I bought what I thought was a wonderful bargain—fifty clothespins for ten cents—and a perfect gift for our nurse. I was sitting on her lap when she opened it and I knew she was disappointed. I also remember how she always said "Christmas Gift" as a greeting, which bothered me, for I wanted her to say "Merry Christmas." Not until years later did I realize what a perfect greeting she was making—God's gift to us of the Christ Child.

Mary Penruddocke Britton

Gifts from the East

---

*For a year and a half I worked in a rural area in the state of Guana-*juato, Mexico. Then in 1953, the bishop appointed me to the Secretariat of Christian Education in Mexico City. Our staff of three was responsible for program and curriculum resources and training events for two annual conferences.

At that time, Mexico had two school calendar years. In the south, December and January were vacation months, and in the north, July and August. Chicabasco was in the south.

One December I was invited to go to Chicabasco, a desert area in the state of Hidalgo. I rode the bus and got off on the highway where the pastor met me. There was no transportation into the village, so we walked about five kilometers carrying my suitcases and school supplies.

I lived with one of the families in Chicabasco. They had no bathroom, no toilet facilities. I had to go into the cornfields to relieve myself. Water had to be brought in almost daily from a long distance. What little water was left over at the end of the day the women poured on their few flowerpots. The federal government had offered the people of this village fertile lands elsewhere, but they refused to move. This was their land. This was where they and their parents and ancestors had been born. They loved the land and would not leave it.

During the mornings we held Vacation Bible School. In the afternoons we visited families and practiced with the children for the Christmas program. In the evenings we held evangelistic services. Time passed quickly for me, and I not only enjoyed the experience but also felt the beauty of the land and of the people who lived in this remote village.

Everything seemed to go well during my time there. The worship service on the last evening was especially uplifting. I was happy, yet uneasy because no word was said about my leaving the following morning, no "thank you" for coming. Nothing. I began questioning my effectiveness. *Had I said or done anything offensive to hurt these people in some way?*

I went to the home where I was staying and packed. In the morning the pastor would accompany me on the long walk back to the highway where I'd get on the bus and return to Mexico City.

When the pastor came for me, I told him I needed to go by the church to pick up a few things. As we walked out of the church, the pastor suddenly caught my arm. "Look!" He pointed toward the east. Three young boys were coming along the dusty road carrying something in their hands.

The boys approached rather bashfully. "Senorita," one of them said, "thank you for coming to live among us. We have brought these gifts for you." As the children offered me gifts of peanuts, flowers, and freshly cut and cleaned cacti, people from the church gathered around us. They appeared suddenly from nowhere, or so it seemed. They hugged me and thanked me for coming to their village. My tears flowed as I expressed my gratitude for their teaching me how to love the land, and for helping me experience the God of the wilderness.

Later, as the pastor and I walked back to the highway, I reflected on the gifts given to me with love and sacrifice. Like the wise men of old, three children had come from the east bearing gifts.

Peanuts were the gold, yellow and expensive. Since the people could grow nothing on their land, the peanuts were a luxury bought with the few extra coins they had saved.

Flowers represented the frankincense, a sweet fragrant offering that delighted the eye and the soul.

Cacti symbolized the myrrh, the bitterness of the hard life in the desert, and the ointment of survival. It not only survives but gives life, for many use it as food. I remember my mother cooking it with onion or eggs or making it into a salad. Delicious!

I was not the Christ Child, but they had seen in me a child of God who came to live among them. And having been in the desert for a while, I was now prepared to go back into the world.

Mary Lou Santillán Baert

The Year We Couldn't Afford a Tree

The year I was eleven, my mother called my older brother and me into the living room and explained that because of our family's financial situation, Christmas was going to be limited. One of the things she felt we really couldn't afford was a Christmas tree.

This was devastating news to me. Intellectually I understood my mother's decision, but in my heart I just couldn't accept it. A tree had always been such an important part of our family tradition and such a special thing for me: I loved making ornaments, decorating the tree, putting my wrapped gifts under it, and anticipating what would be waiting there for me.

I became noticeably glum and made sure my mother and brother knew the reason for my dejection. Mrs. Miller— our neighbor as well as a family friend for whom I ran errands—heard my sorry tale as well. And so did my fifth grade classmates at Madison Elementary. It wasn't that I went around telling everyone, but because I wasn't my usual cheery self the story got around.

The afternoon school let out for Christmas vacation, the teacher called our class together. She explained that my family wasn't going to have a tree and asked the class's permission to give me the tree from our room. In retrospect it was embarrassing, but at the time I was so jubilant about getting a tree that it didn't strike me as such.

That day I went home dragging the tree behind me. We lived about a mile and a half from school, and I remember looking back and seeing the path the tree made in the snow. As I approached our house I started running, shouting my good news ahead of me. When I burst in the front door and asked my mother to help me get the tree inside, she got a strange look on her face. The reason for her look was suddenly clear: there in the living room stood a tree. My mother felt so guilty about upsetting me with her decision not to have a tree that she decided buying one was worth the extra expense.

While I was still ecstatic over having two trees, my brother trailed into the house with yet another. He was two-and-a-half years older than I and had a paper route. The money he made helped supplement the family income. He felt so bad seeing me dejected that he managed to save enough from his earnings to buy a tree.

Word of our "no tree" situation also reached my sister and her husband who had recently moved back to town. They soon showed up with a tree for us.

With the arrival of each new tree, my excitement grew. As we stood in the living room with me insisting we put up *all* the trees, I glanced out the window. Who should be coming across the street but our friend Mrs. Miller and her husband. And what were they dragging behind them? Another Christmas tree!

The year we weren't going to have even one tree, we ended up with five. And we did indeed put them all up: one stood in the living room, one on the porch, one in the dining room, one in the back bedroom, and one between my mother's bedroom and the bath. We had only one tree stand, so we stuck the other trees in buckets of sand, and then got very inventive with decorations. We made colorful chains from the comics in the Sunday papers. We created decorations from clothespins and construction paper. We strung cranberries and popcorn. My brother, who was in junior high, used the tin snips in his shop class to shape ornaments from tin cans. For a finishing touch, we sprinkled Ivory soap flakes on the branches to look like snow.

Some of the trees were sparsely decorated, but that didn't matter to me. All five were up. What began as a gloomy holiday season ended up being my most wonderful and memorable Christmas.

Pj Doyle

Boot Camp Christmas

It was 1967 and time for me to drop out of college until I got my academic act together. Back then those who lost their student status went either into the service or to Canada. My father and uncles had been in the navy, which influenced my decision to join. By the time I got to boot camp it was mid-December, and Christmas Eve soon rolled around.

No one in boot camp was allowed to go home for the holidays, which made for a lot of downhearted guys. At twenty-one I was one of the older recruits. Because of my age, and also because I had been away at prep school and later lived on my own, I figured I was better able to tolerate the loneliness than some of the other guys. I took the barracks' watch on Christmas Eve with the idea I might be able to help those who were having a hard time spending the holiday away from home.

The barracks with its dim lighting was always dreary at night, but on Christmas Eve the gloom was magnified. Light that slanted through the windows from street lamps outside only added to the feeling of melancholy. As I started on my rounds, some of the guys called out "MERR-RY Christmas!" in exaggerated heartiness. But mostly there was silence and forlorn, unhappy faces. When I noticed a guy crying, I'd stop and exchange a few words with him. I especially remember one kid who said, "Would you come and talk to me a while? He was from Georgia and his family was very close. Until he joined the navy, he'd never been away from home. Now that it was Christmas, his homesickness was almost too much to bear.

As the night wore on I talked to so many guys that I felt like Father Riley. I thought about how, through time, there have always been people who've had to work on Christmas and other holidays. I wondered if the men pulling the oars on the emperor's barge and the guys working the salt mines got off for major holidays, or just the emperor's birthday. I thought about the sailors on ship and others in the military and felt a kinship with them. Doing my duty while the rest of the world celebrated Christmas gave me a certain enjoyment. Or maybe it was a sense of pride.

Out the window I saw the lights of Christmas in the hills of San Diego. Here and there a church spire shone brightly. One large building was decorated with lights in the shape of a Christmas tree. I thought about my brothers and sister back home and all that I was missing in our traditional family celebration. Like the rest of the guys, I was lonely too.

On Christmas the navy gave us the day off from our regular duties. We had a turkey dinner with all the trimmings and then spent our time reading or writing letters or just lying in the sun by the wash tables on the sunny side of the building. Even though it wasn't the merriest Christmas I ever had, I went to bed counting my blessings. In 1967 there were things far worse than spending Christmas in boot camp. I could have been in Khe Sanh or some other combat zone. In the grand scope of human history my situation wasn't too bad. God willing, I would have a lot more Christmases and be able to celebrate them surrounded by family and friends.

Pat Riley

Yes, Megan, There Is
A Santa Claus

One year when my little brother still believed in all the magic and make-believe of Christmas, he came home devastated at being told there was no Santa Claus. I rushed to dry his tears and ease his misery. "Oh, but there is a Santa. There is," I assured him. "The kids are just being mean. Santa will come this year just as he always has."

Mother and Dad also turned back the terrible news, winking me into their confidence. So it was on that Christmas—newly fallen in my own Santa faith—that I joined the ones old enough to fib for a good cause. And so too, with a kind of double vision, I looked through the tinsel decorating my beautiful new doll dishes and heard beyond the jingling bells and slamming back door on Christmas Eve and the excited report that Santa had been there and we just missed him again.

All at once I saw these pleasures and their fabrication, the little lies, the myth-making born of love. I also saw how we older ones longed as much as the youngest child to stave off the painful truth; how we wanted to believe and affirm the magic for one more year.

The next year, and for many years following, Christmas was only what it seemed, and I saw how my family mourned when no one believed anymore. And then for a few wonderful years my own daughter, Megan, carried the magic and we all poured into her—the only child in so many ways—the tastes and tales of our Christmases.

When the time came to tell Megan the truth about Santa, I recalled that first Christmas of my own collision with reality. It seemed to me that the moment would be a kind of birth for her, and I wanted it to be gentle. I shut out the tinny music and insistent commercials and in a quiet moment said to her, "Santa is real, Megan, but as you already suspect, he isn't a big fat man with white hair. Santa is the spirit of Christmas, and he comes to you through all the people who love and cherish you. Santa lives in all of us and in you too!"

The two of us then shared a story I had written especially for her. Megan and I are the main characters, and at the end of the story I give her my own teddy bear. The one condition of ownership is that if she ever gets too busy to care for the bear she will give it back to me and never to anyone else. The bear is our deposit of love and for our precious love and for our precious bear we always want the best.

Megan is now twelve, and of all the people I know, she enjoys Christmas the most. She prepares gifts for her relatives and friends months in advance of the holiday, gladly spending most of her year's savings. And I truly believe she looks forward to seeing us open our gifts from her as much as she looks forward to receiving her own.

Lea Hall

Power to Make Us Light Up

After being ordained I spent my first Christmas as a missionary in South America. The mission I served is in Guyana on the shores of the Rupununi River. The Makushí Indians who live along the Rupununi are famous for making poison for darts and blowpipes. The poison—curare—is exported for use as a muscle relaxant in heart surgery. The Makushí also gather balata from which the cores of golf balls are made.

The mission at Yupucari was about a hundred years old, and since its beginning had been served by a succession of English priests. The Makushí—who speak beautiful Elizabethan English—learned the language in the mission school.

I was one of the first American priests assigned to the parish of St. Mary's. Being newly married, I didn't want to subject my wife or myself to too primitive a way of life, so we took a few amenities with us. One was a bathtub, which the Makushí didn't understand at all. Another was an electric generator and fuel to run it because I knew we'd have nothing for light except gasoline lanterns and candles.

The native people, who had never seen a generator before, understood only that it made a terrible noise and threw off a lot of smoke. They were sure it was inhabited by a *kanima*, which is Carib Indian for demon or devil; to the Makushí it was a *kanima* machine. I assured them it was not a *kanima* machine. It was a good machine and it was going to bring light to the village.

The generator arrived about mid-December along with wires, sockets, light bulbs, and a set of twinkle lights. Wanting to hold onto some of our Christmas customs, my wife and I went into the jungle and cut down a small tree. We put it in the middle of what was our living room and decorated it with the twinkle lights.

The Makushí were very curious about how we lived and gathered around our house at night just to watch us. Our house had walls about three feet high, and above the walls, posts to support a large canopy of palms. The night I started the generator and the twinkle lights winked on was the first time any of the Makushí had seen such lights. From the jungle around our house came a mighty "oooooOOOHHH." In the following weeks, Makushí walked many miles to see the twinkle lights on the tree in the middle of the missionary's living room.

Besides the tree lights, we had a single bulb hanging on a wire from the roof. I hung another bulb on a wire in the middle of the beautiful old church that was made from mud and grass. We gathered there at the end of each day for evensong. Although the whole village knew evensong by heart and sang it in the dark, I thought a light would be helpful. Everyone loved the light bulb, and soon no one complained about the *kanima* machine.

A man from the village got the idea that he, too, would like a light in his house. Willy walked dozens of miles to a trading post and bought a light bulb, carried the bulb back, and hung it in his house. But of course, nothing happened. The next day Willy came to me, livid that I misled him. *Why did my light bulb work and his did not? Why did I have better magic than he had?* He was indignant at having walked so far to get the bulb, and *would I please come and fix it for him?*

I told Willy I couldn't fix the bulb because you have to have the generator and the wires and the electricity. I tried to explain how power went through the wire and made the bulb in the church light up because it was connected to the generator; if we didn't have the generator, the bulb wouldn't go on. Finally I accompanied Willy home. And there, in the middle of his house, was the bulb, dangling from a piece of twine. Although I couldn't get Willy to understand why his bulb wouldn't light, I did get him calmed down.

Shortly after my meeting with Willy, it was Christmas Eve. Our midnight mass began with a candlelight procession in the completely darkened church. When it was time for the service, I turned the light bulb on and heard the usual "oohhs" and "aahhs" from the people.

After the service I stood at the door of the church as parsons do and greeted everyone. When Willy came by, he grasped my extended hand. "Now I see what Christmas is all about," he assured me. "We are light bulbs and Christmas sends the power to make us light up."

Willy didn't understand the principle of electricity, but he certainly caught on to what Christ's coming at Christmas means to us.

Richards Wolff Beekmann

To Us a Child Was Born

On Christmas Eve morning my husband and I found out that we were pregnant with our first child. A pregnancy test kit confirmed what we so much wanted to be true. I always thought how wonderful it would be to be pregnant during Advent, and here I had been and didn't even know it! Carey and I were so happy and excited that we told everyone right away. Because we were with his family that Christmas, they were the first to know. Then we started making phone calls to share the wonderful news.

During my pregnancy I experienced God in a whole different way. Until then I had never felt that God was within me; now I did, and I identified with Mary. The Magnificat had always been one of my favorite parts of the Bible. The spiritual experience of God coming to Mary saying, "My child will be within you," and the feelings she must have had when the child moved carried a whole new meaning for me.

Throughout my pregnancy I didn't feel a lot of spiritual support, which I found difficult. The church, like society, didn't seem supportive of the family as an institution, or of women dedicating themselves to being mothers and homemakers. The liturgy wasn't speaking to me about the experience of motherhood either. Even during Advent the readings are not about a woman having a baby. Instead they are about reflecting on our lives and being penitent.

Since Andrew's birth, my whole life has shifted focus. Instead of being in the world of corporate finance, I spend my days being with my son and caring for him. This has changed my perception of what is valuable in life and what life is really about. I grew up thinking life was about deeds I performed and what those deeds achieved in society as a whole. Now my deeds are changing diapers and doing laundry, and I'm very much aware of the significance of them even though they don't get much respect. I remember being in business meetings and thinking, *I can't believe these people are taking this so seriously.* Now I feel that what I'm doing is the real essence of life and hardly anybody takes it seriously.

On Andrew's first Christmas I was amazed at what little importance I placed on gifts. What mattered was people. A really close friend spent Christmas with us. At this point in my friend's life, her only family is her mother, whose mind has failed and she no longer recognizes her daughter. The richness of our Christmas was being together and having Andrew with us. Afterward my friend and I talked on the phone about how wonderful it was to share time with one another and how we wished we lived closer.

This Christmas experience made me think about community and the people I'd like to be around. I used to think about where I wanted to live in terms of geography, or of the profession I could have in various places, or the activities different areas offered. Now I think of community in terms of what would be a good place to raise a child and be a family.

That first Christmas with Andrew we began traditions that we want to be part of our family life in years to come. We took Andrew to the Christmas Eve service. We prepared a Christmas dinner with loving care. Before eating, we bowed our heads in prayer. And very importantly, we opened our home to share the joy and the warmth of our family with a friend.

Janice Lilly

The Gift of Self

In 1944 our country was just beginning to investigate the use of radar in wartime, so all high school senior boys were given a test to determine their aptitude for this specialized field. Because my brother, Don, passed the test with such a high score, he was taken into the Navy as soon as he graduated. When he left for boot camp at the Great Lakes Naval Training Center outside Chicago, he was only seventeen. Just the year before he left home, I had gone to work in Des Moines, so for the first time my folks were left alone. This was traumatic for them because they really wanted their kids to stay at home in Ottumwa, Iowa.

Christmas of 1944 I came home to spend the holiday with the folks. I tried my best to cheer them up, but my mother, who *adored* Don, would have no part of it. According to her this was the grimmest Christmas anyone ever faced in an entire lifetime. There was no cheer. There was nothing. I was beginning to wonder why I had come home. Instead of my being an upper for them, they were a downer for me. It was just miserable.

We usually opened gifts on Christmas Eve, but this year my mother decided there really was no point in doing that. Don wasn't there. I can't remember if we postponed the gift opening until the next morning or what, but it was gloom and doom. About nine o'clock the doorbell rang and we couldn't imagine who would be ringing the bell on Christmas Eve. My dad went to see who it was, and when he opened the door, there stood my brother!

What a surprise, and what joy there was after that. Don had gotten a thirty-six-hour pass, and he rode home on a train that was so crowded he had to stand most of the way.

He would have to leave by six o'clock the next night, but he was with us on Christmas Eve and we would eat Christmas dinner together.

Of course my mother was upset that she had sent Don's gifts by mail and there was nothing under the tree for him, but he didn't care. Just being together—that was the important thing. I was twenty-two then and for the first time in my life I realized there was more to Christmas than gifts. I don't think there has been a Christmas since when I have been hung up on whether or not I had a gift for somebody or whether somebody had a gift for me. What I learned from the Christmas of '44 is that the best thing you can do for another person is to give the gift of yourself.

Dorothy Screeden

Christmas: A Different Vision

If you were to ask me when I first noticed that I get depressed at holiday time, I doubt if I could tell you. One thing that sticks in my mind, though, is Christmas of '76 when I found myself driving through the Great Smoky Mountains on my way north to Mama. I had a black eye, missing teeth, and my small children were in the back seat and kept asking me where Daddy was.

The next few Christmases, spent on AFDC, were just as dismal. Those were the years I stood in long lines at the Salvation Army and other places waiting for a well-meaning, but patronizing individual to hand me my toy ration. Standing in handout lines produces some very strange feelings. On the one hand, you're grateful—glad that your kids will get something for Christmas. But on the other hand, you resent being there and can't shake a vague feeling of humiliation.

You wonder, while standing there, how it can be that in the wealthiest country in the world, there have to be lines for the poor and shelters for the homeless and hungry. You think how ironic it is that there are so many poor and hungry Americans that there aren't enough of these shelters.

More often than not, the attitude of the persons on the other end of the line who give you your handout perpetuates your feeling of inferiority as they glance at you but don't really seem to see you. Too, you notice a difference in the way they speak to their co-workers and the heightened tone of voice they use when addressing you. It's as though you, the recipient, must be spoken to very loudly and words must be clearly enunciated. They seem to be saying, "You're in this line because you're poor and, therefore, you're ignorant."

I stood in those food stamp and toy lines because it was important to me to stay home with my kids during their developmental years. It infuriates me that women with husbands and higher incomes are praised if they stay home with their youngsters, while low income mothers who want the same thing for their kids are condemned as lazy.

I know that many of today's young mothers have careers and send their small children to day care centers or have baby-sitters. Many women wouldn't consider AFDC as an option. But having been raised in a home where my mother worked and we kids had to fend for ourselves a lot of the time, I felt no romance in having a career while my children were small. I didn't want anyone else to raise them.

While on the welfare rolls, I struggled to build up my job skills and self-esteem by taking an occasional class, working temp jobs now and then, and typing manuscripts while I also worked at being a good mother/father. I knew my youngsters would soon be old enough for me to feel comfortable going out to work.

My kids are older now and I am very comfortable going out to work. Still, I hope I will never forget those years. If nothing else, they were character-building for both me and the kids. We were forced to learn certain survival skills.

And though those days are far behind me, when I see a young single mother struggling through the grocery store line, at her wits' end, her kids tired and crying, only to be looked at contemptuously by the cashier when she pulls out her food stamps, I sympathize. I know about the things she's had to put up with all day, all month, all year—the price she's had to pay for being poor.

When my kids were small, I wished I had the courage to do away with Christmas in my house. It's very difficult for black children to see rosy-cheeked white children on TV advertising the toy they can't have. It has the negative effect of making them feel there must be something wrong with them.

65

I'm sure it's no better for low-income people of other races, including those who are white. And it's just as difficult for parents who can't afford to indulge their children. Too often the parents share the child's self-doubts.

And what about the goodwill part of Christmas? Shouldn't it last all year?

I still wish for the courage to tell my kids "no Christmas this year," even though only two are left at home. But when I really start thinking about it seriously, I guess I've had to deny my kids so many things through the years that I'm just not willing to look into their eyes—bright with anticipation of what they'll get for Christmas—and tell them, "Nothing."

"Why not, Mom?" they'd ask.

"Because I hate Christmas."

What about their right to their own individuality? Their right to love the things I don't care for? I prefer to do my gift giving throughout the year, when I can afford it or when I feel motivated to give, rather than at Christmas, when gift giving is prescribed. My kids give throughout the year, too. But they enjoy Christmas as well. Why should I spoil it for them?

Carolyn Holbrook

The Year We Made Our Gifts

My side of the family had grown tired of holiday shopping, and buying gifts for our many relatives was costly. So for Christmas of 1974 we decided to try something different. Instead of buying presents, we all agreed to make them.

At home I suggested to my husband and kids that we knit most of our gifts, and they went along with the idea. Gene made a knitting board, and Julie and Jay, who were still at home, worked with me knitting scarves for their cousins. David, who was in his first year of college, took his turn at the knitting board when he came home on weekends. After we finished eight or ten scarves, Gene made a great big board on which we knit four afghans for the women in the family.

For the men, we made batches of candy and caramel corn. My dad especially likes candy turtles so we made those for him.

I don't recall all the gifts we exchanged that year. But I do remember that my sister gave us bouquets of dried flowers. And my sister-in-law, who has a talent for sewing, made bathrobes or lounging jackets for everybody. The robe she gave me was a particular favorite of mine and I wore it for many years.

A gift I remember especially was the one my brother made for my mother. That year my parents had moved from the farm and were spending their first Christmas in town. For years my mother wanted a fireplace in her house on the farm, but she never got one. So in my parents' new house in town, my brother built a fireplace for her out of materials we all helped buy. The sad fact was that after the fireplace was built, she never got to use it.

Shortly after Christmas that year, my mother went into the hospital. She was diagnosed with cancer and died on March 9, her birthday. After that, we never again made Christmas gifts for one another. Even though it had been a very satisfying experience, doing it again would have been a sad reminder of the last Christmas Mom was with us.

Carine Schroeder

The Light Is Here

I am of Dutch descent and until age seventeen I lived in Holland.
Christmas there was celebrated differently from the way it is
in the U.S. Christmas was considered a holy day, but Saint
Nicholas Day (observed on December 6) was for gift giving.
Saint Nicholas arrived by boat from Spain and always rode a
white horse. He was dressed in bishop's clothes, wore a
mitre, and held a staff in his hand.

The traditional belief was that Saint Nicholas arrived
several days early, and it was a custom to put out hay,
raisins, and cookies for his horse. In turn, Saint Nicholas left
a gift of candy or something else small—things similar to the
Christmas stocking gifts that are traditional in the U.S.

After the gift giving on December 6, we prepared for
Christmas, which lasted two days and was strictly a religious
observance. The manger scene was the predominant Christmas theme in the home.

What I loved most about the holidays in Holland
were the days between Christmas and New Year's Day.
Throughout that time it was the custom to wish a wonderful
Christmas and a Happy New Year to everyone you knew:
family, neighbors, and friends.

Every house was literally loaded with wonderful
food, and wherever you went, evidence of loving preparation
was visible. It was a real community time, and the gift was
the sharing of food and time and being welcomed into people's homes and having them come to ours. The warmth and
feeling of unity was wonderful and quite a contrast to the
commercialism that has attached itself to so much of the
Christmas observance in the U.S.

Christmas, though, did not become truly meaningful for me until after I had what would probably be called a conversion experience. It happened after I came to the U.S. All of a sudden my eyes were opened to who God is and to the realization that God loves me. Prior to this experience, God was out there somewhere and very remote. I was afraid of him because if he killed his own son, what would he do to me? But somehow, through the church, through Christian friends—and I'm certain by the grace of the Holy Spirit—I saw who Jesus was. I understood that he had come for me just as he had come for everyone else. For the first time in my life I had the awareness that God lives in me.

After my spiritual awakening, Christmas was, and has remained, a true celebration. The light I saw on the tree was the light that had come into the world. To this day when I decorate my tree and turn on the lights for the first time, I feel wonder and awe. My breath catches and I know that, *yes, the light is here.*

Ludy Turner

Peace at Last

My father shouldered a .22-caliber rifle during Christmas of 1941 and practiced marching in our living room. His voice was deep with patriotism as he commanded himself through a routine of right, left, and about faces. He expected to be in the army soon and wanted to march well. My father was a tall man with dark and wavy hair and a smile he didn't often show because his teeth were very crooked. Though my mother cried at the thought of him going to war, I imagined him a hero.

But my father was not to wear a uniform or be a hero on the battlefield. His voice reflected his disappointment the day he thrust the .22 to the back of the closet and informed us that he had been classified 4F. Subject closed!

4F? Unfit for military service? My father? I began to be ashamed of him and wondered if the whispers about his being a drunk were true because of his sometimes unsteady walk. In a country stirred with patriotic fervor, a man declared 4F was labeled a sissy, a coward, not really a man. I couldn't imagine how awful it was for him to be rejected, unable to fight for his country.

Soon my father left our small town and found work in a defense plant in Vandalia, Ohio. He came home only occasionally as the war progressed. Though I was always glad to see him, in my young heart he seemed a failure. I was a shy and self-centered boy who yearned to have a hero for a father. We seldom talked, but on one of his visits my father tousled my hair just as he was leaving on the Greyhound and promised, "I'll get you a bike as soon as I can." Then he walked unsteadily to the door of the bus headed for Ohio. I imagined he'd been drinking and that image of him grew in

71

my thoughts as one Christmas passed and then another. The bike never came.

By the Christmas of 1944, I was eleven and had turned much of my love away from my absent father to an uncle in the marines who was awarded a purple heart while fighting in the South Pacific. The following spring my father came home unexpectedly and invited me to walk downtown with him. I thought maybe we were going to get ice cream. Instead we stood quietly by ourselves on the sidewalk outside the restaurant. The huge Greyhound whooshed right up to the curb and I wondered if my father was leaving again. The driver hopped out, took a ticket from my father, and opened the cargo door. There, in the midst of the luggage, was a bike.

"It's yours," my father said. "The only one I could find."

It didn't matter that it was a used bike, or painted red with a careless brush. It was my first bike! I grasped the handlebars that angled like the wings of a soaring gull. The leather seat had several knife slits, but I was already imagining wrapping it with friction tape. I'm not sure I even said thanks, because the roaring engine of the bus pulling away drowned whatever my dad and I said.

My father and I never did get to truly know each other. His progressing illness was eventually diagnosed as multiple sclerosis, and—although that explained why he was 4F—life at home became more and more stressful. At eighteen I joined the air force to get away. While I was serving overseas in Japan, my father died of complications of the disease he'd had for so many years. By the time I got home, he was buried. Buried, too, were my memories of our relationship.

Thirty years later, when my mother died shortly before Christmas in 1985, we returned her to the small town cemetery where my father was buried. It was an unusually warm day for December, and I could not seem to leave this wonderfully peaceful place that reminded me of my history. All around me were stones marking the graves of people I'd known in childhood. After my wife went to the car, I stood there alone. Ashamed. Guilty. Facing long unfinished business. My eyes blurred as I said good-bye to my mother and then asked God and my father to forgive me. Then a great peace came over me and I realized it was time to leave.

I am now the elder in my family, the keeper of memories. Every Christmas Eve I take my father's Elgin pocket watch out of the glass bell display case in our living room. I wind it, set the time, and reflect on the thirty years it took me to make peace with my dad. Each Christmas I recall something else good about him that I had buried in my heart. I think of him now, not as a man ravaged by disease, but as a father who loved me and did the best he could.

Herb Montgomery

Gifts from the Heart

Whenever my husband and I are asked about a memorable Christmas, we both recall the same one because it has stayed very much in our minds. It was the Christmas when we were a struggling young couple and especially broke. We had five daughters ages seven to two, and no money with which to buy gifts.

We couldn't let Christmas go by without presents for the girls, so Irv came up with the idea of making something for them. He made a whole kitchen set: a stove, a sink, a cupboard. He also made two board games. One was a ring toss on a slanted board. The other was also a slanted board in which he cut holes and designed a game that you played by rolling golf balls into the holes. He did a beautiful job on each gift and the girls were absolutely delighted.

The presents Irv made were in our family for years and years and became extremely well used. That Christmas started a tradition for us. Every year after that Irv handmade one gift as a remembrance of how poor we were one Christmas and how much love we had.

Kay Carr

Morgan and the Decals

The Christmas our daughter, Eartha, was four she wanted a Big Wheels—one of those colorful plastic tricycles in which you sit low to operate the pedals. Our son, Morgan, was about a year and a half, so we decided to get Eartha a Big Wheels and Morgan a mini Big Wheels that didn't have pedals. It was just for toddlers and you pushed it around like a walker.

The Big Wheels came unassembled, and after we finally got the kids to bed on Christmas Eve, I still had to put the gifts together. This was a job I dreaded because I am not very mechanically inclined. I can do basic mechanical things, but assembly and reading instructions and making sense out of diagrams is not my forte.

It was late when I went to the kitchen to start my task. But when I looked at the diagram, the assembly wasn't as complicated as I thought, and to my surprise, I had all the necessary tools. Although the job took time, everything went pretty well. I was quite proud of myself and went to get Doreen, who was reading in another room. There the bikes stood on the kitchen table, fully assembled and with no parts left over.

Doreen examined the bikes and said they looked fine. In fact she said they looked just *great*, only I had left the decals off. Indeed, I had done just that. I felt so good about getting the bikes assembled that I overlooked the decals.

During the next hour I discovered that putting the decals on was the hardest part of the whole job. Everywhere there was a space, it seemed a decal was supposed to go. The decals had to be peeled off a paper and then matched just so to the space. With Doreen's help I finally got them all on and we put the bikes under the tree.

The next morning when the kids got up and saw their Big Wheels, they were very excited and wanted to ride. The bikes are best for outdoor play, but that year it was bitterly cold and our Kentucky farm was covered with snow. The next best thing was going around our big living room. Morgan made the circle once, then got off his bike and began studying the decals. The more he looked, the more fascinated he became with them. After three or four minutes of looking he sat on the floor and—not paying attention to his other presents or anything else—proceeded to pick off all the decals on his mini Big Wheels.

As I watched Morgan, it struck me that his picking off the decals was an appropriate image for Christmas. On Christmas we celebrate the fact that God sent us Jesus who turned the world upside down. And there was my son turning my world upside down by picking off every single one of the decals that I had worked so hard to put on.

Tom Duley

Two Dimes for Nicholas

When I was thirteen, our family moved from St. Louis to Min-
neapolis. It was a move that none of us wanted to make. My
parents come from large families and most of these relatives
still live in the St. Louis area. We have a very close extended
family, and before our move we often got together, especially
around the holidays.

The first year after we moved, we made several trips
back to St. Louis. It soon became apparent that we could not
keep doing that; we had to make a life for ourselves in a new
place. My dad decided it might help if we got involved in
charitable work, so he contacted Little Brothers Friends of the
Elderly. That was in 1972 and every year since, our family
has spent Christmas, Easter, and Thanksgiving Day serving
dinner and providing entertainment for people who would
otherwise be alone.

The Little Brothers is a nondenominational organization whose purpose is to alleviate isolation and loneliness
among the elderly. Once the organization befriends an older
person, that friendship is maintained until the person dies.

The first Christmas our family was involved in only a
small way at a group dinner: we poured coffee, cleared
tables, and helped clean the pots and pans. I was assigned to
stand at the door and welcome people. I gave a lot of hugs
and began to know people's names. Soon those we set out to
help became part of our larger family.

Each year our family did a little more. My parents are
especially dedicated to the Little Brothers organization, and
have done a lot of behind-the-scenes work that they are too
humble to take credit for. Fifteen years ago, our family assumed responsibility for serving from 75 to 125 elderly on the

holidays at a downtown site. The Little Brothers organization supplies the food and decorations along with a list of senior citizens. My father organizes the kitchen crew to produce a hearty holiday dinner, while my mom arranges tables and flowers to create a festive atmosphere. Volunteers transport our guests and join us in serving the family-style meal and providing entertainment.

The first Christmas we were involved, my brothers, Mark and Craig, were ages seven and eight. Years later Craig recalled that experience in a paper he wrote for college entrance. In "One Cup of Coffee" he told how as kids he and his brother sat on the steps not knowing how to act around all these "old people." Then he noticed a lady looking for someone to pour her a cup of coffee. He did not see anyone nearby to do it, so he found a full coffeepot and filled her cup. The person next to her needed coffee too, and my brother slowly found his niche.

Over the years, both my brothers have developed confidence in dealing with the elderly and in expressing their care for those who are so often isolated. At some point in the passing years, Craig started playing Santa Claus at the Christmas parties, and he is the best. With each gift he delivers from the Little Brothers, he also gives a warm hug. The seniors look forward to Santa's arrival, in part because they lack the human contact that is so important. Mark, too, found a special way to serve the elderly. For years he has spent Christmas day in the coat room, making sure that the seniors know that their belongings will be secure while they enjoy the party. He has collected many stories from elderly friends who decided to spend a little extra time with "that nice young boy" in the coat room.

Several years ago I married and now have three children of my own. I have taken more of a back seat at the holiday celebrations, and my sister, Maureen, now helps my mother organize the parties; she acts as the master of ceremonies throughout the day's activities. My husband, Bill, has become an integral part of the kitchen crew. Every third year I miss the Christmas dinner because we travel to Detroit for Bill's family reunions. My parents tell me that the seniors always ask about me, or any other family member who is not at the Little Brothers party. Our elderly friends probably keep track of us more than we keep track of them. And I do miss them when we are unable to celebrate Christmas Day together.

My two eldest children are now four and three years old and have been going to the Christmas dinner with the Little Brothers since they were infants. They create a lot of excitement because the elderly people love having children around. Nicholas was only two months old the first time I took him to a Christmas dinner. One gentleman wanted to hold the baby, and of course I let him. After the party he came up to me and gave me two dimes and told me to put them in Nicholas's piggy bank. I cried because I am sure the man was just going from meal to meal and that was the only change he had in his pocket. As for those two dimes, they are still in Nicholas's piggy bank.

Donna M. Watz

The Bob Hope
Christmas Special Live

In 1969 I was a corpsman on the hospital ship USS Sanctuary off
the coast of Vietnam. On Christmas morning I was assigned
the task of taking nineteen injured marines to see Bob Hope's
Christmas show on Freedom Hill. Although the marines had
a variety of injuries, they were all able to walk. Early in the
morning we were ferried into the boat landing at Da Nang.
From there I commandeered an army truck that got us to
Freedom Hill.

Those of us on board the Sanctuary had been given a
preview of the show. The night before—on Christmas Eve—
Hope's troupe was on an aircraft carrier near the ship. They
called and asked if we would pull alongside. Then they
hopped on a chopper and came over: Bob Hope, Connie
Stevens, Neil Armstrong, Teresa Graves. They wore no
makeup and put on an impromptu show. Connie Stevens
sang without accompaniment and had us all hanging onto
every note.

For the Freedom Hill performance, the nineteen
marines and I had second row seats from which to watch the
show that folks back home would see on television. The
jokes, the singing, the dancing—it was very upbeat and a
great diversion from the fighting even though we couldn't
put the war out of our minds completely. Overhead a chopper in obvious trouble was giving off a lot of smoke. On
stage, Bob Hope directed the camera crew to get that action
on film just as he directed them to pick up the fire and shells
going off in the distance.

My mission after the show was to get the marines back to the ship. I found a truck to take us to the docking area where I got a call out to the Sanctuary. They sent a boat to pick us up. When we boarded, I had only seventeen of the nineteen marines I left with. The officers on the ship were incensed that I couldn't account for everyone, but I figured that one corpsman losing two marines out of nineteen wasn't a bad average considering how many bars we passed.

We got the men back to their wards and saw to it that they had a late supper. Only then did I realize that I hadn't eaten anything since an early morning breakfast. By that time the chow line was closed so I went down and found a friend who was a cook. The best he could do for me was a peanut butter and jelly sandwich, which ended up being my Christmas dinner. All in all, it was a Christmas to remember.

Bob Brooks

Christmas at Home

My father loved Christmas—all of it. The cards with the family photo, the Christmas Eve slide show followed by the family gifts, the turkey dinner, and next morning, brunch that came after the opening of Santa's gifts, the visits by friends, and the playing of Charades, which we shared on Christmas night with the Langmo family. If the weather permitted on Christmas night, Dad took out his accordion and we serenaded friends, our breath freezing in the cold air, the night as still as the fabled night in another small town that we were remembering.

Every year Dad took one or two of us kids along to pick out a Christmas tree, and it was always the scraggliest one in the lot. Our mother groaned when we brought it home. But I found it touching that Dad, a doctor, knew instinctively which tree most needed a place to fit, was crying out the loudest for love and warmth.

Decorating the tree usually fell to the two youngest girls, Annie and Mary. They also picked out the slides, afraid that if they didn't the carousel would be loaded with the more plentiful shots of Jimmy, Billy, and me, the three of us having been around longer. But all of us were kids when it came to Christmas morning. Until late into our high school years, we waited expectantly at the bottom of the hall stairway, cat-like, eager for the door to be opened when we would be allowed to pounce upon "our" chairs, filled with gifts.

It's difficult to distinguish among the Christmases I knew as a girl growing up in a small town. They were so much the same. Therein lay the beauty. If you believe, as I do now at the age of thirty-five, that much of life cannot be predicted, and that most of the world operates in a barely disguised chaos that can break open anytime, then what my father created in his series of traditional, harmonious, utterly dependable holidays rivaled the making of a work of art—except life is always transient, fleeting, and changeable.

Our Christmases changed when the family changed—or more exactly, when individual members of the family grew up, left home, had experiences that were not always pleasant, and my father encountered years of turmoil that took a toll on his spiritual and physical health. But the routines remained; I seldom missed Christmas. At Christmastime, we still opened gifts in the order that we had established, and the tree looked just as scraggly as ever.

One way or another, we found our paths again. Dad started enjoying the smaller things in life, appreciating whatever fame and time remained to him, writing as much as possible. Mom relaxed when Dad relaxed. I missed my father's next-to-last Christmas, spending it instead in the remarkably similar household of his sister in Connecticut, since I was living in New York City. But all around, life had settled down. Things remained the same. Therein lay the beauty.

My father died a few days before Christmas in 1986. "He probably did it on purpose," said Annie, "so he would be sure we remember him." I can hear my father say, "Well, it worked, didn't it?" In his room before he was wheeled off to his final heart bypass operation, when he was still coherent, I said as brightly as possible, "I've already bought your Christmas gift. You'll have to be here to open it." Knowing my financial situation, he quipped, "You can return it."

We kept the rituals even that year. My long secularized family showed up in church for the first time in years, to say good-bye to my father. I think that, for some of us anyway, a resurgent belief also returned that added a poignancy to the holidays that had been missing too long. On Christmas

Day, we opened Santa's gifts, ate our brunch, and got together with the Langmos that night. We tried to do everything exactly the way Dad had liked. He had picked out the tree before he died, and we thought it was beautiful. Mom opened her gifts that Dad had chosen beforehand, and I gave the book I had bought for him to one of my brothers. We laughed and we cried, but through the Charades, we celebrated our Christmas as we always had.

Since that year, as in years before, the ritual of Christmas has brought us together no matter how few people show up at home. Everyone tries to make it. I suspect that as the four who are now married begin their own family Christmases (from no grandchildren, next year there will be three), the same traditions will be handed on.

Wherever I go on Christmas Day, in my heart I journey to the home that I knew once as the surest thing on this earth. There my father's grave collects the snow, which can never cover the spirit of his life.

Jody Nolen

Christmas Spice

My dad is hard to buy for. Sure, you can always get new clothes, but how many pairs of 32 x 32 button-fly Levi's does one man need? Ditto with shirts. As for leisure pursuits, he already owns four cribbage boards and the cupboard in the dining room is cluttered with playing cards, both standard and pinochle. So, the man is set.

I thought I had the gift dilemma licked when I lent him a copy of a Louis L'Amour novel to read on the plane after a visit. He finished it before he left the house. I was dumbfounded: my dad, who in all my twenty-six years I had never seen with a novel in his hands, liked to read. For a readaholic daughter, this was wonderful gift tidings. But when I gave him a boxed set of Zane Grey and it went un-read, I realized that books wouldn't do it. With his Norwegian work ethic, he had to be *doing* something. And reading books wasn't it.

Christmas has a way of coming even if you haven't purchased that last gift. I wandered through the aisles at Target—if a frenzied jog behind a speeding cart can be called a wander—looking for ideas. I bypassed men's clothes and was detouring around a large display of special items in red and green gift boxes when I saw the Old Spice.

The sight of it opened up pathways to my past. I sniffed as if I could catch the spicy scent right out of my memories. Or was one of those carefully sealed boxes leak-ing? I know my eyes were.

When my sisters and I were little, we bought Dad the same thing every Christmas: socks, hankies, Old Spice, with an occasional wallet thrown in when his wore out. We fought over who would give the treasured after-shave. So much

more exotic than white socks and hankies. So much an insep-
arable part of Dad, a smell that permeated his hugs. Fresh,
clean, like the boy in navy dress blues in the picture on
Mom's dresser.

My gift to Dad that year wasn't large. It wasn't expensive. It didn't strain my budget. When he opened the box,
everyone in the big front room—uncles, cousins, sisters,
friends—gave a little cheer. "Old Spice," Dad said, giving me
that smile that crinkles his eyes. For a second, the scene of
Christmas Present wafted away on the scent of after-shave,
and there I was in Christmas Past, a little girl who had given
her father one of the necessary luxuries of life.

When I blinked my eyes, I was back to now, back to
being a grown-up. But I was still a daughter, and he was still
Dad, and Old Spice was still the perfect gift. I even threw in a
pair of socks.

Laurel Winter

An Empty Place

My mother died in August the year I was seventeen. The first Christmas after her death was extremely painful. My father, sister, two brothers, and I were not known for being especially gentle and loving with one another. But that whole Christmas season we were so careful of one another's feelings it was like walking on eggshells. We each sort of sat on our sadness and sat on our sorrow, hoping no one would notice. We seemed to think that if we didn't admit we were dying inside, then we wouldn't be dying.

We tried to carry on family traditions as though nothing had changed even though everything had, and nothing would be quite the same again. The Christmas tree stood in its usual place in the corner of the living room. And as usual, Father—who was very protective of the light bill—decreed that whenever we had the tree lights on, all the other lights in the living room had to be off unless someone was reading.

On Christmas Eve our family was all together and waiting to go to church. I recall walking from the kitchen through the dining room and into the living room. The only lights were those on the Christmas tree, and the only person in the room was Grandmother. She sat in a chair beside the tree looking like she was off in space somewhere and crying softly. In that unguarded moment, the expression on her face was one of such absolute sadness and total misery that I thought, *We are not going to survive. I can't stand my own pain. And I can't stand anyone else's pain. Things will never be right again.*

Instead of finding comfort in the warm glow of the Christmas tree lights, I felt that they were mocking me. "This is the season to be merry," they taunted. "Everyone else is having a good time. Too bad about you."

The lights took me back to Christmas ten years earlier when a call from the hospital notified us that Mother was very sick and might not live. Her blood pressure was perilously high, and at the time there was no effective treatment. Then, too, I felt taunted by the Christmas tree lights: "Merry, merry, merry," they said to me. "That's what you're supposed to be, not sad and worried."

For days after I heard the news about Mother I was rigid with fear. I remember feeling like a vase full of water, afraid that if I was not careful the water would spill all over. After she came home from the hospital, the initial terror passed. But during the ensuing years my brothers, sister, and I lived with the fear that any misstep on our part, any chore left undone, any bit of contrariness might raise Mother's blood pressure and kill her. Even though she died of a heart attack, I think we each felt at least a little bit responsible for her poor health and worried that we had somehow contributed to her death.

The first Christmas after Mother's death was the hardest. Maybe that's because the many traditions surrounding the holiday season made her empty place so noticeable.

In time, my grief lessened and I got on with my life. Many Christmases came and went, and when people said they got depressed or edgy or uptight during the holiday season, I didn't identify with them. Christmas was no problem for me, or so I thought.

Only during the past year have I come to understand that the experiences related here forever influenced the way I feel about Christmas. Now I realize that I have always protected myself by not getting too involved in the holidays. I don't decorate my house because it's a big chore. Although I enjoy get-togethers, and the family feeling, and being in touch with people I may not see at other times of the year, I don't invest a lot of emotion. I think this all goes back to my childhood experiences. They led me to believe that the best way to protect yourself is not to pay a lot of attention to the holidays and to keep your expectations low, because if you give Christmas a chance, it will kill you. Or at least it will leave an empty place in your heart that you can never quite fill.

Mary Meade Elliott

The Year I Got Everything I Wanted

I was a child during the height of the Depression. Throughout the thirties there were not a lot of jobs and my father, like so many other men, had difficulty finding work. Christmas at our house was usually devoid of gifts, or at least of toys. My brother, Noel, and I received scarves and mittens and gifts like that. An apple and maybe another piece of fruit filled the stockings we hung on the fireplace.

One year shortly after Christmas, Noel and I were approached by the newspaper routes manager and asked if we would be interested in delivering papers. In those days the money from one route wasn't worth the effort, so when we discovered there were four routes we each took two.

Every morning Noel and I got up when it was still pitch black outside. Whether it was snowing or raining or thirty below zero, the papers had to be delivered. A lot of the people on my route had huge dogs—Dobermans, mastiffs, and one dog whose breed I don't remember but he was big as a buffalo. I was terrified of him, not because he was mean but because he liked to leap on me and lick my face.

With the four routes, Noel and I each made about fourteen or fifteen dollars a week. By the time the next Christmas season came around, we had saved a good deal of our money. We decided to get everyone the gifts we'd never before had the money to buy, and to buy gifts for ourselves.

My brother and I went through the stores buying everything we really had an eye for and could afford. We got our mother a scarf and a pretty handkerchief and a fancy vase—frivolous gifts that boys think their mothers will like. For my father we bought gloves and a hammer and things like that because he worked with his hands a lot.

When it came to shopping for ourselves, Noel and I knew our wants very well. We bought a fort and lead soldiers and miniature cannons and little airplanes. We had the whole battlefield. We bought modeling clay and Lincoln Logs and Tinker Toys and other playthings that would last a long time. When our shopping spree ended, we wrapped the gifts and stacked everything under the tree.

On Christmas Eve when our family gathered around the tree to open presents, Noel and I had the most incredible time. It was the Christmas we got everything we wanted. I could tell that Mother disapproved a little. Times were tough and to spend so much money on gifts was shocking. But she must have been able to see how pleased my brother and I were that we were able to buy gifts for everyone, and she did not ruin our good time by expressing her disapproval.

Although we lived in a nice neighborhood, we weren't as well off as the other families. That year the neighborhood children were incredibly impressed with all the gifts Noel and I got. Of course, they didn't know that we bought them for ourselves.

In retrospect, all my Christmases as a child were very good. My mother was an excellent cook, and groceries were reasonable back then. All the relatives came to our house for dinner. They played cards and listened to the radio and talked and argued and discussed. Christmas Day was always interesting even though it was sometimes pandemonium. The people who celebrated Christmas at our house are all gone now and missed very much. In looking back I am able to appreciate that their presence in our home was more important to me than the presents under the tree.

Armand Maanum

On Duty

I was just beginning my nursing career, and had worked for about three months in a Boston hospital when I decided to work on Christmas Eve. Then I'd catch the early morning train for New Hampshire and spend Christmas with my family.

As I was finishing my evening shift, the supervisor came down the long corridor of the large old hospital. "We're desperate on 4E," she said. "The nurse who was scheduled has the flu. Can you work a double shift?" I agreed to work, thinking I could still catch the eight o'clock train. The timing would be tight, but it was possible.

By the time I got to 4E, the evening nurse had already left, so I got no report. I had never been on the unit before. It was just one big room with sixteen beds all filled with very, very sick men. Seeing what I had agreed to, I immediately called the supervisor, who didn't answer her page until much later. It was eleven at night, men were groaning, and I was alone.

I stood in the middle of the big room looking at IVs running too fast and seeing other problems that needed attention. Clearly I had to prioritize, but what was the most important thing I should be doing? Just then the intern showed up. He was the first person in sight to dump on. I told him I didn't know what I was doing, I didn't know how to do what I was *supposed* to be doing, and I was absolutely panicked. At that point, one of the patients started yelling, "Nurse, nurse. . . ." I don't know what I looked like, but I wear my emotions on my face. I fixed my eyes on that intern. He responded by turning on his heels and leaving. For the first time in my life I uttered obscenities, using words I didn't even know I knew.

92

I went over to the patient who'd called out and managed to take care of him, all the while thinking *what do I do next?* Just as I turned around, the intern came back with his resident. The two of them were absolutely marvelous. One of the patients with a colostomy had problems and the intern cleaned him up. He and the resident stayed with me all night and we set up a team system. About five in the morning, one of the patients had a respiratory arrest and the intern and resident took care of him.

At seven o'clock the day nurse was supposed to come on, but arrived late because of an unexpected snowstorm. When I finally got off duty, I went to the Director of Nurses' office ready to rant and rave, only I couldn't find anyone to let loose on. So I walked to my apartment through ankle-deep snow and without any boots, muttering all the way. Suddenly I remembered I was supposed to be on the train and my family was waiting for me. When I got home, I called my sister and explained that I wasn't going to make it home for Christmas. The only train out that day had left.

No sooner had I hung up the phone than it rang. The nursing office was on the line wanting to know if I could come in at three that afternoon. They wanted to be sure to get me before I went to sleep!

Actually, I did go back to the hospital. And my shift was in 4E again. Then I stayed on and did a double shift Christmas night. That year began a pattern in my nursing life: every Christmas after that I chose to be on duty. In a way the decision hurt, because I never got to see my nieces and nephews on the holidays. But for me it was a matter of growing up and accepting the responsibilities of my profession. I figured that if someone was going to work on Christmas, the patients deserved to have it be a nurse who really cared about being there.

D.M. Boulay

An Orange in the Toe

*When I was a little girl, the children in our family raced down-*stairs on Christmas morning to see what awaited in our stockings. We knew there would be underwear sticking out of the tops, which was always embarrassing. But once we got past that, the delights unfolded. We counted on receiving M&M's and "oohed" and "aahed" over them just as we did each item we pulled out. There were such treasures as pencils and tape and little notebooks—gifts I think Dad bought at the drugstore on Christmas Eve. One gift remained at the bottom of the stocking, and we didn't have to guess what it was. Always and *always* we found an orange in the toe.

I used to think only children in *our* family got an orange in the toe of their Christmas stockings, but I have since learned that other kids got one in theirs, too. I believe the tradition began during the Depression when there wasn't money to buy anything else. In a way that's disappointing because for a long time I thought the idea originated with my dad, who seemed to be in charge of the stockings.

All families have Christmas traditions, and not all of them are happy. But if we take what is good and happy from our backgrounds and pass it along I think we are passing along a part of ourselves. Now that I have a family of my own, my two sons always find an orange in the toe of their stockings. When they ask, "Why is it there?" I say, "Because my parents did it for us."

Just as I always found underwear sticking out of my stocking, so too do my sons. This year one of them said, "Mom, do you really *have* to put underwear in the stockings?"

"Not all traditions are fun," I told them. "Some are annoying!"

If you were to ask my sons about the holiday traditions in our family, they would probably come up with a hundred or more. I wonder which of them they will carry into their adult lives. If they have children of their own someday, I will be curious to see whether they find an orange in the toe of their Christmas stockings. And to see if maybe—just maybe—there is underwear sticking out of the top.

Lynne M. Deming

A Christmas Well Spent

My idea of a well spent Christmas occurred in 1990. But to understand why this Christmas was significant for me, it is necessary to know a little about my background.

I am of Chinese ancestry, and one of eleven children. During the Revolution in China my parents fled to India. By the time I was born they had moved to that section of India which had become Pakistan. Growing up there in Karachi, we were immersed in Muslim culture. When my older sister, Lucia, became a Catholic at age sixteen, the rest of us children followed. Although my father did not accept the faith until many years later, he wanted this for us because it gave him a sense of security. We got our schooling from the church and he knew that if anything happened to him, the church would take care of us.

In 1973 I came to the United States as a foreign student and have lived here ever since. I celebrated Christmas with different families and in different ways and always left feeling empty. It seemed that I was doing what convention demanded without ever getting at the true spirit of Christmas.

Then in 1978 I entered the convent. Christmas was nice, but there was always so much to do. So many prayers, so many schedules to keep, so many formalities, and so many singing practices. It was like being on a bus that kept going and going, and all I wanted was to get off. This is not to say that I didn't enjoy what had to be done, but only that it was not my preferred way. I often wondered about my attitude toward Christmas and how I would spend it if I had a choice.

Then came the Christmas of 1990.

By then I had come to a point in my life where I felt free of external obligations. I realized that it is not what I do, but how I feel inside that matters. No longer was I feeling the pressure of what I ought, or ought not do.

Preparations for Christmas that year were low-key. We all helped decorate the tree and the convent. Initially, we planned a large dinner, but instead opted for a brunch that relieved us of having to spend so much time in the kitchen. It was like the Martha and Mary complex: either you spend all your time doing this and that, or you decide to do a little and enjoy the wonder of the Incarnation.

That Christmas I had a deep awareness of God and of my own being. It was not a time of doing and going, but a time of being present to God and to the people around me. There was no disharmony, only perfect contentment and grace.

Over time I have come to appreciate simplicity and now know that only some things matter: all else is pure busyness. What is important is the present. I realize that I do not have control over anything. My role is to tend to my tasks and leave the rest with God and the workings of the universe. It is not being Martha, but simply being Mary. Enjoyment and contentment come from living now and truly feeling grateful for everything that has happened and will happen in my life. The Magnificat finally became real to me: to be favored and given such peace and serenity is grace upon grace.

Christmas Day was quite simple and ordinary. We did nothing more significant than stay home and enjoy the feast of the Incarnation. This is a feast in which heaven and earth are wed and over the whole world there is hope and renewal. Our God is here to stay.

Liang, Lee Mei

My Christmas Miracle

At eleven-thirty in the evening the phone in our hotel room rang.
My brother was on the line. "Mom is sick and we've taken
her to the hospital," he said. "You better come home right
away."

Our family was in Duluth, Minnesota, at a hockey
tournament in which our three sons were playing. My husband and I quickly made arrangements for the boys to stay
with another family and started the three-hour drive home to
St. Paul. All I could think was, *I lost my father last year and now
my mother. I don't know if I can handle this.*

At the hospital my two sisters greeted me crying. My
brother said, "Beware, Sharon. Mom's very sick and the doctors don't know if she'll pull through."

When I went into the intensive care unit, my mother
was extremely restless and thrashing about on the bed. But
that was not to be her condition for long. Doctors diagnosed
her as having encephalomeningitis and she soon lapsed into
a coma. That's when our family vigil began. Day and night
my brother, sisters, and I were with her. One of the doctors
told us to keep talking to her. "Talk about the weather, your
families, anything that comes to mind," he said. "What you
say doesn't matter. The important thing is to talk and try to
stimulate her."

I stayed at my mother's bedside during the day. At
night I slept in the visitors' lounge where the television was
always on. The holiday shows and the carols and the talk of
Christmas reminded me of home and the fact that there were
no presents under the tree. But then it was a year when gifts
weren't very important. The only present my sons really
wanted was for their grandma to be well and out of the

hospital. The song "I'll Be Home for Christmas" tore at my heart.

The longer my mother was in the coma, the less hope the doctors held out for her. They said that if she did wake up we could expect her to be severely disabled both mentally and physically. On December twenty-third—the eighth day of the coma—my brother, sisters, and I met in the chapel with the hospital chaplain and our minister. We lit a candle and stayed there praying until the flame went out. Then with tears streaming down our faces, we asked God to take our mother because she wouldn't want to live if her mind was gone and she couldn't function on her own.

We all left the chapel and went back to intensive care where our Lutheran minister gave my mother the last rites and anointed her with oil. After that we held hands over her body and sang "Jesus Loves Me."

The next morning was Christmas Eve day and nothing in my mother's condition appeared to have changed. She lay still as death and her breathing was shallow. I began talking to her as usual even though I had lost all hope of getting a response. But then I saw her right eyelid quiver. I ran to the nurses' station and told the nurses there what I'd seen. They rushed back with me. When they saw that my mother was starting to wake up, someone rushed to get the doctor. Before he got there, my mother opened one eye.

Hardly able to believe what was happening, I bent over her and said, "Mom, this is Sharon."

She looked bewildered. I pulled down the hospital mask we always had to wear when we went into her room. "Mom, this is Sharon," I repeated.

"You *are* Sharon," she said. And that was the start of her recovery.

By midafternoon, twenty-four of Mom's relatives stood outside the glass-enclosed intensive care unit. When they waved to her, she waved back even though she didn't understand what all the fuss was about. It seemed impossible to her that she had been in a coma for nine days. She thought she had been sick overnight and was waking up the next day. What concerned her the most was getting her cookies to a Christmas party she was giving with her friend.

Mom required physical therapy and used a walker for a while. But in a few months she needed only a supporting arm or a hand to hold. Within a year she was on a bowling team and was taking two-mile walks. Her only aftereffects were a slight loss of hearing in her left ear and a left eye that's a little bit lazy. The doctors involved in her case were astounded by her recovery.

All this happened in 1978. Today my mother is an active seventy-five-year-old and the heart of our family. For me, December twenty-fourth will always be the day my mother came back to life. She is my Christmas miracle.

Sharon Wess Montgomery

Christmas in Katmandu

Wanderlust can descend at any season of the year. Since I am at present unmarried, and my children are grown with families of their own, it is not difficult to shift dates for the exchange of presents and other customs to accommodate trips. So it was that I traveled to Katmandu, Nepal, during the Christmas season.

Nepal is the world's only Hindu kingdom. Officially, however, it is made up of ninety percent Hindu, five percent Buddhist, and three percent Islamic followers. In my guidebook I found no mention of Christianity. Proselytizing is prohibited by law in Nepal with a lengthy jail term awaiting offending parties, both the converter and the convert. Still, I was alert for signs of the Christmas celebration.

On December twenty-fourth, along with a small group of travel companions, I checked into a five-star hotel situated about fifteen minutes from the city center of Katmandu. Imagine my surprise to see a myriad of brilliantly lit Christmas trees appear in the halls and corners of the hotel, with the same sparkling cheeriness they display back home. Strings of Christmas lights extended from the roof to the ground on all sides of the hotel. To top it off, on Christmas Day a waiter came to each of our rooms to present us with a cake made in the likeness of a Yule log artistically frosted with brown and trimmed with a green frosting bow.

Although Hindu and Buddhist temples exist in all sections of the city, I did not see any churches. Again, I was surprised when, on Christmas morning, I wandered to the lower level of the hotel where a small shopping center attracted foreigners. Of course all the shops were open for business. As I peered into one doorway, I saw a clergyman in his white robes visiting with a group of men and women. He gave me a big smile and I was on the point of entering the room when it occurred to me that perhaps it was a meeting. Later I discovered that the clergyman was conducting a Christmas service. I supposed he could not come out to invite me in because he might be disobeying the law.

Though I was disappointed at missing services, my fellow travelers and I celebrated our special day with a private Christmas meal.

Lila Gundersen

Gifts to Cherish

I knew that the last Christmas in the house where my three children had grown up was going to be very difficult for me, and I was sure it would be for the kids as well. My divorce was final, and in the spring when my youngest son turned eighteen, I would have to sell the house. I'd been too ill to work that year, so there was no money to buy presents for the kids. This troubled me greatly.

On Christmas Eve, the kids were scheduled to go to their father's house where they would get presents from him. They were then to come home where I would have nothing for them. I thought and thought about what I could do. Finally I hit on an idea. Why not give them things in the house that meant a lot to me and to us as a family? Since I was moving in the spring, this was an opportunity to go through the house and pick out items that had particular meaning for each child.

The first gift I thought of was for my daughter, and it was an easy choice. She loved my rosebud necklace that once belonged to my mother; the beads of the necklace were actually made from rose petals. For my oldest son I chose a hand-painted china cup and matching cake plate that he especially liked. My younger son longed for his grandmother's collection of Indian head pennies, and that seemed just right for him. I then chose one more gift for each: a desk from childhood, a 12-gauge shotgun, a special pottery jar in which we'd kept school lunch money.

Although I was sure the kids would like what I chose for them, I wasn't yet satisfied. Something in this gift idea was missing. Not until Christmas Eve, when the kids were at their father's, did I come up with the idea that had been eluding me. Just giving them gifts was okay, but a treasure hunt would be so much more fun. I quickly hid the gifts, then wrote the clues needed to find them.

When the kids arrived later that evening, I gave them their clues and the search was on. My daughter's clue led her to the Christmas tree and the inside of an ornament where she found the rosebud necklace. My older son's clue led him to the china cabinet. And this—the only clue I remember in its entirety—led my younger son to a spider plant hanging from the ceiling:

> Grandma scrimped and squirreled away
> > pennies for a rainy day.
> Now yours to keep where 'ere you rove,
> > a spider guards this treasure trove.

My children are now grown and when I visit their homes, I see the gifts I passed on that Christmas I didn't have money to buy presents for them. It gives me great satisfaction to know they cherish these things that are part of their past and mine.

Bonnie Smith-Yackel

Home for the Holidays

When I was a sophomore at the University of Nebraska, I took a train home for the holidays. Home was Fargo, North Dakota, and I had to transfer in Minneapolis where my city relatives gathered at the depot to meet me. Then it was back on another train for the final leg of the long trip, which was to take about another five hours.

Once the train left the city, telephone poles and barns with silos nearby and fields of stubble crusted with snow glided past the window. At small towns along the way, we lurched to a stop, letting off and taking on passengers, then forging on toward my destination. The closer we got to Fargo, the more anxious and excited I was to be nearing home. The conductor who passed through the car calling out stops said we were right on schedule. That was the case at least until we got to Barnesville, just thirty miles from home. I don't know if we got switched to a sidetrack so another train could pass or what, but in Barnesville we sat.

And we sat.

And we sat.

At that point in the trip, Fargo seemed like a snowball's throw away, yet it might as well have been on another continent considering that I was on a train that refused to move. I fidgeted and fumed and kept looking at my watch, wondering how much longer we'd be stalled when my brother, Jimmy, and a friend of his burst into the passenger car. "We found her!" they yelled. "We found her!"

Everyone turned to stare at us.

"Come on," Jimmy said. "I got a car and we came to get you." He and his friend grabbed my suitcase and bustled me off the train, their words tumbling over one another as they asked how I was and said they were so glad to see me and told me how they just couldn't wait any longer.

"We found out the train was in Barnesville," Jimmy said as he slung my suitcase into the trunk of the car. "So I said, 'What are we waiting for? Let's go get her.' "

I glanced back at the parked train. Passengers looked out at us, their faces framed in the lighted windows, and I imagined then thinking, *Look at her. Isn't she lucky? She's going to be home soon.*

We leaped in the car and raced off, laughing and carrying on. By the time we got to Fargo, everyone who had gone to the depot to greet me was waiting at my house. I was home and it was good.

Mary Lou Brooks

The Year I Got a Second Gift

A Christmas I remember very well was when I was ten years old and my brother, Johnny, was seven. My father had been out of work a great deal and there was very little money for Christmas gifts. Mom told Johnny and me that we were going to get only one gift, and we could have whatever we wanted so long as it wasn't too expensive.

That year all the girls were wearing medallion pins to school. I wanted to be like the others so I asked for a pin. My brother, of course—always so thoughtful—asked for traps because then he could trap rabbits to put food on the table. I remember being very annoyed with him because he always managed to be a nicer person than I.

When Christmas Day came, there were two gifts under the tree for Johnny and two for me. I was astounded and overjoyed. The first package I opened contained the medallion. It was a very pretty pin, and I wore it for many years. The second gift was my first grown-up slip. Instead of having wide straps, it had narrow ones that adjusted. Instead of being cotton, the material felt like silk, only I'm sure it wasn't. Rayon maybe, but it was wonderful.

I appreciated the gift so much because I knew how poor we were that Christmas and what it meant for my mother to find the money to buy a second gift. But the slip was important for another reason too. It was a sign that my mother recognized me as the responsible and helpful person I tried to be. That was the best Christmas ever because, even though we were poor, Mother gave me great joy.

Dee Ready

On the Other Side

My dad battled leukemia for almost ten years. He was a very religious man who felt it was important to be a member of a church. Two years before his death, my parents moved to southwestern Florida and joined an Episcopal parish there. As a member of this new congregation, Dad involved himself in hospice and other kinds of outreach for which he could draw on his own experience with illness.

I intended to spend Christmas with my parents, but when Dad was hospitalized with pneumonia on December 22, I went a couple days earlier than planned. My first thought when I saw him with the breathing tubes was that they had to be out by Christmas Eve, otherwise he couldn't take communion. But as time passed, it became clear that Dad might not make it. Yet I just could not believe that God would let him die before Christmas. It seemed so unfair.

Ever since I can remember, our family has gone to the Christmas Eve service at church. But this year—with Mom and all five of us kids gathered at Dad's bedside—we decided to break with tradition and stay at the hospital. When Dad died at six-thirty in the evening on Christmas Eve, we were with him. Afterward we went back to the apartment and the priest came over to talk to my mother about the funeral service. He then left to go out of town for Christmas, and long into the night my family and I shared stories and tears.

On Christmas—the day before Dad's funeral—our family went to church together. Our eyes were red from crying and we had the disheveled look of people who are too distraught to care about appearance. Clearly we were in distress, yet not one person in that church acknowledged our presence or bothered to ask us why we were there. The topic of the sermon was the Incarnation. Other than that, I don't remember anything about the service. After it was over, we shook hands with the clergy and left to wait for the funeral the next day.

More than anything else in my life, my experience that Christmas taught me what it is to be church. Mostly I learned what church is not: it is not a place that says, "I'm sorry if you have a problem, but I'm sure you can take care of it yourselves." It is not a place where you ignore strangers. It is not a place where you talk about the Incarnation but don't see the Christ in every person.

That day I made a vow to myself about being church to others. I vowed there would never be a time when I didn't greet someone new to the congregation or approach a person who was obviously hurting and say, "Do you need someone? Can I be that person?"

At Dad's funeral I was still deeply saddened that he had not received communion on Christmas Eve. Doing so was very important to him and something he had done every Christmas since he was old enough to receive. But then I remembered that a metaphor for Eucharist is being at the heavenly banquet. Dad was in fact at the banquet, but not on our side of the table. He was on the other side.

Louise Thibodaux

Oh Christmas Tree

It was too beautiful to be alone on a Currier & Ives kind of night when snow glistens across the hills like glitter on a Christmas card. But it was dusk and I was alone as I drove through the valley to the farm. My purpose: to cut a tree.

A wooden sign proclaiming "XMAS TREES—CUT YOURSELF" marked the turn to the ancient white house where warm light from frosted window panes provided a beacon. I parked beneath a naked maple and left my car. The steps to the porch glimmered with a fine glaze of ice. Before I had a chance to knock, an old woman who carried eight decades well flung the door wide. Her blue eyes stared through wire-rimmed bifocals speckled with flour dust. The fragrance of baking bread, cinnamon, and nutmeg escaped into the night. At her feet stood the ratty little mongrel, Valentino. As I stepped into the house, I recalled the first time my husband and I came to this farm. Valentino was just a pup.

The woman ushered me into the kitchen and asked if my husband was fetching the saw. I pretended to struggle with the zipper on my down-filled vest, took a deep breath, and admitted that my husband had left me. I'd come alone.

Hot coffee splashed on the oak table top and the woman apologized as she set the blue willow china down. I don't know whether it was due to my revelation or the spilled coffee, but I felt a violent wave of anger wash over me. The anger I felt toward my husband's abandoning me with three kids, with stretchmarks, with a mortgage owed into the next century. The anger at my own cowardliness— not wanting to tell an old woman I saw once a year that I was

110

a failure. The anger that I kept pent up all fall for the sake of frightened children.

She wiped the spilled coffee with a washrag. The silence was filled with Bing crooning, "Tis the season to be jolly. . ." from a radio atop the fridge. When the woman spoke, her voice was soft and thoughtful, without a trace of the judgmental or reproachful inflections I'd become accustomed to. Tears I'd fought all day began to pool.

She pulled her chair next to mine and handed me a handkerchief that smelled like spring. She listened while I talked about my fears, my lost dreams, how I dreaded the coming holidays and the forced smile that proclaimed I was fine. I'm strong, I said. I talked while she listened to the words I'd held captive. And so it went well into the evening.

When I got up to leave, she refused the twenty dollar bill I tried to press into her hand. She took off her glasses and wiped them on her apron, offered to get her coat and boots and keep me company while I sawed down the tree.

I was struck by her generosity: her way of letting me know she understood how much I'd dreaded this simple chore. But it was something I had to do myself. She described the location of a perfect tree while Valentino eagerly escorted me to the door. A brief embrace and then I stepped into the cold air. The radiance of a thousand stars danced in the clear sky while light from a pregnant moon reflected off the hard-packed snow, creating long shadows across the landscape.

I left my purse in the car, and grabbed a flashlight and the rusty saw. Determined, I hiked into the quiet woods, pausing at the split rail fence to watch a startled doe zigzag across the meadow. To the west through the pasture gate, I continued toward the evergreen cove. On a knoll to my left was the tree she'd described: tall and proud, it stood alone on a hill in the night.

Susan L. Stoker

111

The Gift

Pearl Harbor had just been attacked, and we'd heard President Roosevelt speak to us over the airwaves on our new Motorola radio. I was seven that year and a nail biter. I had no real understanding of what was happening in the war or in my family. I only knew that my heart was anxious to get through this annual wild and noisy Christmas Eve. If I'd been super good—and Santa really listened when I told him what I wanted—I'd awake tomorrow to find a Flexible Flyer sled and a set of Lincoln Logs under the tree.

This particular Christmas my favorite uncle and his wife came to our house. In his hand, Uncle Al held a small gift wrapped in beautiful red paper circled with a green ribbon. And it was for me!

Uncle Al owned a bar in a skid row area and was the one relative our family talked about in whispers. They called him a ladies' man and other things. I didn't care what people whispered about him. Here he was. And I was eager for him to finish greeting everyone and hand me the gift. Finally he and my aunt took off their coats and gave them to my mother who carried them into the bedroom. Instead of giving me the gift, Uncle Al shook it just beyond my reach and said, "This is for my special niece."

My shy response was a hand-covered grin as I looked into his smiling face and twinkling eyes. I loved him. As far as I was concerned, everybody loved him. Except of course my spinster Aunt Esther, who didn't like the way he acted toward women.

Our upstairs duplex was filled that night with the entire bunch of "outlaw alkies" as my father called them. Loud conversations turned into hollering and arguing about Roosevelt and the dirty sneak attack on Pearl Harbor.

When my mother returned from adding the coats to the mountain already on the bed, Uncle Al handed me the gift. I ripped off the paper with no regard to being a dainty lady as my Aunt Esther was trying to have me become.

Inside the wrapping was a box and inside the box was a soft leather case, which I quickly unzipped. The magical contents were a dozen bottles of bright nail polish and several metal tools that I assumed had something to do with making hands beautiful. In that instant, I promised myself never to bite my nails again.

Mother snatched the case away from me. "For crying out loud, Al, the kid's only seven! Take it back!" She rezipped the case and thrust it at him. Right then I promised God I wouldn't ask for anything else in my life—not even a Flexible Flyer—if only I could have my gift back.

Uncle Al smiled and said, "I want my favorite niece looking beautiful." He picked up my hand and kissed it before giving back the leather case. "After her nails are just a bit longer they'll look great with a dab of color on them."

My mother glared at him for a moment, then said, "Only cheap women wear nail polish." There was that familiar and scary look in her eye. "Oh well," she said, "let her keep it. I'm leaving for a refill." Then Uncle Al winked and said, "Happy holiday, sweetheart."

I ran into the bedroom and leaped atop the soft mountain of coats. (Only many years later would I understand that mine was an alcoholic and dysfunctional family system.) That night I clutched Uncle Al's gift to my heart and thought how great it was to know that someone I loved believed I was beautiful. I fell asleep on top of the coats as the crowd began singing "O Little Town of Bethlehem."

Donna Kline

A Magical House at Christmas

As youngsters, my two brothers, sister, and I grew up with my mother and our grandparents. Grandmother's father had been an ambassador, so she traveled and studied all over the world. Although we were not a well-to-do family, we kids were introduced to the cultural side of life. A lot of emphasis was placed on reading, art, and poetry.

At Christmas the whole family was very much into things you make yourself, and the joy of food and customs. Grandmother made strudel, our traditional gift to friends. She rolled out the pastry on our huge dining room table. We kids contributed by walking around the table putting glasses and bowls on the side of the pastry as it stretched thinner and thinner. Grandma said the pastry had to be rolled thin enough to read a love letter through it. Only after the pastry met her high standards did she cover it with apples, cinnamon, raisins, and the other good things that went into the making before she rolled and baked it. Once out of the oven, Grandmother's fabulous strudel was ready for gift giving.

Cookie making was also a family endeavor. My mother, an artist, drew shapes that my grandfather made into cookie cutters in his workshop. Grandmother baked the cookies and we kids helped decorate them. My mother and grandmother were, however, the master cookie decorators. They once were featured in the newspaper because their decorated cutouts were so outstanding.

A long-standing family custom involved making things for the tree. Around the base of the tree stood little houses that my mother constructed. At night, in the darkened living room, our tree glowed with small candle

114

lights, and it was all very magical. The year I was eight, my mother made a chalk drawing of me gazing at the tree with an enchanted look. Then on Christmas Day the whole family sat around the dining room table, and together we wrote this poem:

Our Christmas Tree

Our Christmas tree's a fairyland,
    a song in notes of gold.
A little girl can see such things
    when she is eight years old.
Cobwebs spun of shining threads
    hold mirrors that reflect
The gauzy wings of tiny beings
    her eyes alone detect.
They sing a little tinkling song
    as in and out they flit,
While busy bringing wishes true
    their secret plans they knit.
Deep branches form green caverns,
    that hush in mystery.
The happy bright surprises
    in store for you and me.
But amid all this gaiety and cheer,
We must not forget why our tree is here.
We will think of the beautiful
    birthday of yore
And remember and live by the
    things it stands for.

The family gift that year was the picture of me that my mother drew and the poem we composed. At Christmas ours was a magical house, and it was wonderful to live there.

Karel Ann Hannon Laing

Holiday Blackout

At sixteen, I haven't experienced as many Christmases as a lot of people, and I can't remember very well the Christmases I have experienced. But there is a fairly meaningful one I remember the year I was eight.

Actually the memorable aspects didn't happen on Christmas, but two or three days before. It was night and I was home watching a movie on TV. Suddenly the picture blacked out, then came back on, then blacked out and stayed blacked out. So did the lights—and the lights in the houses on either side of us. I remember the overwhelming darkness. I couldn't find my way around until my dad came with a flashlight and led me downstairs.

The entire family grouped around the Christmas tree in the living room. There was my mom, my brother, my dad, and me. The phone still worked and when it rang my mom took the flashlight and dashed off to answer it. She learned that all the houses on our side of the street were blacked out, as well as a fifth of the town. Still, I felt it was unfair that we didn't have power when the houses across the street did.

We had one battery-operated radio, which my dad tried to tune to a local station to see if there were any announcements about the power outage. Unfortunately the dial didn't work very well, so it took him awhile to get one of the lite rock stations. We finally found out that there was a problem at the local power company. Fortunately this was the year my dad planned on having his office Christmas party at our house, and he had purchased many large candles for decorations. We lit most of them to light up the living room. My dad sat in a chair and read the newspaper. My brother and I took the flashlight and went up to my room to get an anthology of children's stories that we'd had for a year or so. Then my mom, my brother, and I curled up with a blanket on the couch and Mom read us Christmas stories. With the decorations and all, we kept in the Christmas spirit.

Eventually the lights came back on. I think I tried to catch the end of the movie I'd been watching. (I've seen it once or twice since, and don't feel I missed much.)

When I look back at that blackout, it strikes me as surprising that I never once worried about freezing because the heat was off. I know that we had a kerosene space heater, but I don't remember using it. I guess this was just an example of my young, trusting behavior and the faith I had that my parents would protect me from harm.

Devor M. Barton

The Long Way Home

In 1969 I was assigned to Fort Devens, a small army post near Boston, for specialized training that would result in a tour of duty in Vietnam. When training ended, most of my buddies lived close enough to Devens to go home for Christmas. My family lived at a distance and a three-day leave didn't allow enough time for a visit, so I planned to spend Christmas on the post. Because of a field operation I'd been assigned to, I hadn't even been able to send off the gifts I had bought for my family and friends.

After breakfast on December 23 I was sitting on my bunk getting gifts ready to mail when a buddy swooped in and started tossing things into a duffel bag. He told me the company commander was handing out five-day passes. We could get military hops from a nearby air force base. Thinking how great it would be to deliver presents in person, I quickly packed my gear and grabbed a pass.

By the time I reached the air base, most flights had left. But there was one to Rochester, New York, which suited me because I could hitchhike the rest of the way home. Once I got to Canada it would be easy because Highway 401 was the only major road running from Montreal to my home in Windsor.

With no time to read the route of the C-130 transport, I found myself flying first to Maine, then to Greenland, and finally to Rochester! With thirty hours of my pass already spent, I made my way to the New York State Thruway and stuck out my cold thumb.

I didn't get picked up until 10:00 P.M., or I should say pulled out of a snowdrift, and got a ride to Buffalo. There I crossed the river and passed through customs without a hitch. I got my next ride at a traffic light. The driver was headed for a Christmas party at a Canadian Army Legion Hall. He said a truck driver at the party was going to Hamilton—my next destination—so off we went.

The Legion Hall was typical of most organizations dealing with veterans: not much color and hardly any signs of life. At a small table sat a bunch of depressed looking people who surprisingly turned out to be a friendly crowd. Soon I had a good meal in me and met the truck driver who took me on the road again.

By 3:00 in the morning I was standing alone under a bridge outside London. A snowstorm off the lake had nearly closed the road. Although I had only a hundred miles to go, it seemed like a million.

Half an hour passed and the only vehicles to go by were two snowplows going in the opposite direction. Here it was my last Christmas before Vietnam, and it had to be spent like this. I was cold, tired, and lonesome. With each falling snowflake my hopes faded. At my side was a bag full of presents for those I loved, and in my pocket was a pass that time was eating away.

Looking down the road, I spotted yellow specks. At first the specks were dim in the falling snow, but as they came closer I made out the headlights of a van. I held out my thumb and prayed that the driver wouldn't take the off-ramp. He didn't, and the kind soul who stopped helped me finish my trip to Windsor.

When I got home, the house was dark except for a night-light glowing in the living room window. I opened the door quietly and Snoopy, our old dog, gave a low warning growl. Then he came over, sniffed my wet boots, and picked up my identity scent. After taking off my coat and putting my presents under the tree, I lay down on the sofa. Snoopy hopped up and covered my feet.

As I watched the gas flames dance along the jets on the old furnace, I began to feel the importance of being in the right place. I laughed to myself when I thought about a time years before when I drove around dressed like Santa and gave out presents. I wondered if it was as hard for Santa to make it home as it had been for me. And if it was, then no wonder he only made his trip once a year.

J. P. Roberts

To Make a Difference

I work full time during the day and teach adults in a community education program at night. One stormy December evening I hoped the weather was severe enough to get my class cancelled. No such luck. Instead of staying home and baking Christmas cookies as I wanted to do, I layered up with warm clothes and stepped into the dark, frigid night.

As I tried to get my protesting car started, I wondered why I kept on teaching. The pay was lousy, my evenings weren't my own, and who knew if my classes benefited anybody? Countless times my family and friends heard me say, "I've been teaching for fifteen years and quitting for eight."

When I arrived at school, I found the first two doors locked and had to walk all the way around the building before finally getting in. Still annoyed that the class hadn't been cancelled, I was yanking off my boots when an attractive, smiling man in his mid-twenties appeared in the doorway and said, "Is this the 'Getting Along with Others' class?"

I said it was, and putting my annoyance aside, welcomed him. He exuded enthusiasm and cheerfully helped me rearrange the tables for better class interaction. The class began at 6:30, and when I took roll I found out the young man's name was Dale and that he was taking the class to find out if his recent divorce was his fault. His ex-wife said he was hard to get along with and he wanted to know about that.

Throughout my lecture Dale hung onto every word, yet wasn't taking notes. I found this unsettling. *If he was so interested, why wouldn't he want notes to refer back to?* At the end of the three-hour class, students left quickly because of the bad weather. Dale, however, lingered and helped me get the room back in order. Then in a soft, hesitant voice he said, "You might have noticed I didn't take notes."

"Yes, I did."

"I wanted to," Dale said, "but you used words I couldn't spell and didn't understand." He went on to say that he had been a "smart" kid who didn't study in school because he was going to work with his hands. Who needed all that school stuff, anyway? He became a mechanic, married, had a little girl. As time passed he realized that he could hardly read or write. This was hampering him in his work and hurting him as a husband and father. "My divorce cost me my wife and daughter, who I won't get to see at Christmas," he said. "As I listened to you tonight I could tell you are a caring person who might help me. Do you know anywhere I can go to get help with my reading and writing?"

I didn't have an immediate answer, but I told Dale I'd dig up some information for him. He vigorously pumped my hand and with a broad smile said, "God bless you! And Merry Christmas!" Then he was gone.

My class was a one-night session, so I wouldn't see Dale again. The adult ed program had a strict policy that all class lists be turned in and I didn't remember Dale's last name. I called the community ed director and told her my situation. She was not authorized to give me Dale's telephone number, but she said she'd see what she could do. In turn, she called the director of the basic skills program who said that anyone who wanted training had to call the program; the program didn't call a person and say, "I hear you don't read or write. May we help?" She finally persuaded him to bend the rules one time and call Dale.

A week later my home phone rang about 10:30 in the evening. It was Dale and he was so excited that his words tumbled out. He had just gotten home from his first class and it was everything he wanted. "Thank you. Thank you," he said. "I know this is going to change my life."

That experience changed my life too. Every time I think I'm going to quit teaching, Dale comes to mind. When we teach we have an opportunity to make a difference in people's lives. But how often do we ever find out about it? Dale let me know that I made a difference in his life, and it was the best gift I got that Christmas.

Sharron Stockhausen

Something for Gisela

My then-wife, Gisela, was newly arrived in this country from Germany. Though short on cash, I wanted to make Christmas the best ever for her.

Gisela had been washing our thirteen-month-old son's diapers by hand without complaint. Earlier in the week, I'd gone to Sears and arranged for credit to buy a washer and dryer, which were to be delivered on Christmas Eve. When they arrived, Gisela saw the appliances being unloaded from the delivery truck, but did not know they were for her. She thought the landlord, who lived below us in the duplex, had ordered them.

I went down to watch the deliverymen and discovered that the stairwell was too narrow to get the washer and dryer into the basement. The appliances I wanted for Gisela had to go back.

With shopping time running out, I hurried to Sears and explained the situation. Yes, I was told, I could use my line of credit to buy anything I wanted. Once I got the go-ahead, I went through the aisles like wildfire, filling two carts with purchases. I loaded everything into my station wagon and went home. Rather than take the gifts upstairs then, I waited until later.

After Gisela and I had lovingly wished each other a Merry Christmas at midnight, I went into the kitchen and got the hammer from the closet. Then taking dishes from the cupboard, I put them in the sink and began shattering the mismatched odds and ends given to us by my grandma.

At the sound of the crashing dishes, Gisela came flying in the kitchen. *"Mensch! Bist dir verruckt!"* she cried. "Are you crazy?"

"Wait a minute," I said, grinning, and broke a few more. Then I went down to the station wagon and brought up a complete set of chinaware. Gisela loved everything about the dishes. That was my first of many trips. Each trip up the stairs I brought a new item: toaster, blender, waffle iron, electric fry pan, and more. By the time I finished, Gisela's eyes were a little glazed, her smile a little fixed. Even without the washer and dryer, it was a Christmas to remember.

Oh yes, I got a raise at the start of the new year. Then we got a diaper service.

Jack Dukes

When the Healing Began

Because of the alcoholism in my family, Christmas was always a painful experience in my growing up years. Once I married, I wanted Bill's and my Christmases to be very different. After we had children, we never went to his parents' home or to mine for Christmas because I wanted control over the day and what was going to happen. We had some good Christmases in our family. They weren't all good, but they were superior to mine growing up.

After thirty years of marriage, Bill died of cancer, and I really dreaded the first Christmas after his death. I didn't want to be alone with just my two daughters, so we accepted an invitation to spend Christmas with my sister and her family. At the time, she had a small child, and children always bring special joy to the holiday.

My sister had much the same feelings about her childhood Christmases as I, except that she continued the family practice of having a dinner on Christmas Eve and then going to midnight services. My daughters and I went to her house for the dinner. A number of relatives were there and all of them knew this was a painful time for me. I felt that my every move was being watched. Once when I went to the bathroom someone knocked on the door to see if I was all right!

After dinner we all went to church. It so happened that the rector had been my spiritual director at Cursillo three months earlier. I had poured out my heart to him, so he knew that I was having a very rough time. When he came to me at the communion rail, he administered the bread, then knelt and kissed my forehead. It is something I will never forget.

Following the service, I went home and went to bed. The next morning I literally could not get up. I stayed in bed until about four o'clock in the afternoon. I think it was a period I had to go through, but at the time I didn't realize what was happening. I thought I was physically ill, when in fact I was hurting so much emotionally that I couldn't function. It was a painful Christmas, but it was also a good one.

In the years since Bill died, I never had a Christmas tree and I gave all the ornaments to the children. But this past Christmas I decided that next year I am going to put up a tree. To insure that I won't change my mind, I went to the after Christmas sales and bought all the decorations I'll need.

That kiss on the forehead the first Christmas after Bill's death began my healing process. But it has taken me ten years to get to the point that I can put up a tree. Maybe the healing is now complete.

Anonymous

View from a Window

No Christmas goes by that my memory doesn't take me back to my grandmother's house. It was a huge, white frame place with green trim and porches on the first and second stories. Aside from the water tower, it was the tallest structure in town. The house stood on a large corner lot in Claremont, Minnesota, which according to the 1930 census had 399 residents.

For an important part of my growing up years I lived in that house with its stone steps and porches, its red oak banister and six bedrooms, its attic with *National Geographics* dating back to 1890, and a captain's walk on the roof where you could look out and see the flat terrain of Dodge County in all directions. The Christmas out of which all my other pleasant holiday memories grow was when I was five.

I was still an only child, and at seven o'clock I had to take my leave of the grown-ups and go upstairs to bed. My room was the one in which my dad had been born, and I was to sleep in a brass rail bed that my grandmother kept covered with a white crocheted spread. I slid beneath the blankets and pulled them up to my chin, but no heaviness came to my eyelids. The drone of adult conversation punctuated with laughter drifted up from downstairs and added to my wakefulness. But mostly I couldn't nod off because just thinking about the gifts to be opened the next day and the fun that lay ahead started my heart racing.

I climbed out of bed, and in the darkness, made my way to the window. Outside the world was pure and white. In the golden glow of a street light on the corner, snowflakes that looked incredibly big and soft and delicate sifted down from the sky and added to the trackless snow already deep on the ground. Perfect little mounds of snow capped the fence posts, and ridges of snow delicately outlined the wide-spread branches of the butternut trees. It was a scene of such beauty and tranquility that I have never forgotten it. Whenever I want to quiet myself and feel inner peace, I think back to what I beheld as a five-year-old looking out the window of my grandmother's house on Christmas Eve.

I spent at least fifteen Christmases of my life sleeping in that same room in that same brass bed. Sometimes it snowed on Christmas Eve, and sometimes it didn't. But even when it did snow the scene in my memory was better than the real thing. Although my family moved from Claremont, we returned often for visits until my grandmother died. Then the house was sold to people who seemed to love it almost as much as I had.

In 1979 my father died, and on the day before Christmas Eve, we brought him to Claremont to be buried. The new owner of Grandmother's house invited the entire funeral party for lunch. Afterward she took me through the house and even up to the attic.

I noticed that the family was still using the dresser with the secret drawer—a drawer no one had yet discovered. When I pressed the hidden button, the drawer popped out and in it were rocks and bottle caps I had put there as a small boy. The brass rail bed was stored in the basement, and the woman pointed out something else she thought might interest me. It was "The Little Museum of Natural History" in which I had enshrined rocks, fossils from the creek where I loved to play, butterflies, and moths. Pleased as I was that she had respectfully saved it these many years, I declined when she asked if I wanted to take it with me. The view from my window that Christmas when I was five was memory enough of a place that had been such an important part of my life.

Frederick Blanch

Everything I Hoped It Would Be

During my engagement I considered getting married in the spring or summer when there are typically a lot of weddings. Then I thought about a Christmas wedding. I envisioned how Christmas was for me as a child: the warmth of family, the anticipation that sent chills up my arms, the excitement that is so hard to recapture as an adult.

As I got older, Christmas always fell short of my childhood memories. Even though I approached Christmas with the same high expectations, they were never quite realized. I wanted my wedding to recapture the dream of what Christmas used to be. Bob and I set the date for the twenty-seventh of December. Our wedding day was crisp and clear, the ground covered with fresh, clean snow.

So often in the hustle and bustle of Christmas the message of peace and hope gets lost. But on my wedding day the busyness was over and everyone was ready to relax and participate in both the solemnity and joy of the occasion. The ceremony was candle lit, simple but elegant. We chose black, ivory, and red as our colors; red roses decorated the church.

In my family I am the youngest of eight. My brothers and sisters had left home and most lived in distant places. Only rarely did we all get together, but everyone came to my wedding. My father died when I was nineteen, and seeing my mother there without him brought some sadness. Still, I had this really special feeling that I was reliving my childhood experience of grace and love in the presence of family and friends. I felt enfolded in blessings and warmth by the people who meant the most to Bob and to me; my Christmas wedding was everything I hoped it would be.

Mary Greig

The Skeleton Christmas Tree

*Back in the early thirties when I was nineteen, a friend and I trav-*eled halfway across the country to study art at the Pratt Institute in Brooklyn, New York. It was the first time either of us had been away from home, so everything was a big adventure.

Pratt was mainly an engineering school, but it also had a very fine art department, and both my roommate and I were taking commercial art courses. The institute did not have the usual dormitory housing, so students lived off campus in little apartments in the area. My roommate and I found a third floor efficiency walk-up, and though it was tight for space, it met our need for a place to live. When the cold weather set in, we found that our apartment wasn't just warm; it was extremely overheated and the air was very, very dry.

At Christmas break, all the friends my roommate and I had made at school went home. However, we did not go anywhere. Neither of our families could afford the tickets for the long train trip home. We were both accustomed to big family celebrations, so the prospect of spending Christmas in a tiny Brooklyn apartment made us feel terribly lonely and downcast.

To bring some cheer into our lives, we went out and bought a small Christmas tree about three or four feet high. Then we improvised a stand and decorated the tree with great care. We strung cranberries and popcorn and even splurged on a string of lights. In order to plug the lights in, we had to run an extension cord across the living room floor.

Our tree added a festive touch to an otherwise dreary holiday away from home, and we were both pleased with it. Then one day as my roommate walked across the living room, her foot caught on the extension cord. The tree toppled. With a running leap, I quite amazingly caught it before it hit the floor. But the tree I held in my hand was far different from what it had been moments earlier. Although the decorations were undisturbed, not a single needle was left on the tree. The warm, dry air of our apartment made all the needles fall off. The branches were completely bare!

We were not about to start over, so we just made do with the skeleton tree. Whenever I think of that year in Brooklyn, I always recall our little tree strung with cranberries and popcorn, and one string of lights, but naked without its needles. What a sad, funny Christmas it was.

Elizabeth Hannon

Christmas at Aunt Nancy's

My dad had a sweet, eccentric older sister named Nancy who we always went to visit on Christmas Eve day. We had eight kids in our family, and I was the oldest. First it was just me going to Aunt Nancy's. Then me and Joe. Then me and Joe and Bill. Then me, Joe, Bill, and Ann, and on it went.

Shopping for gifts to take to Aunt Nancy was a big and important part of Christmas. My dad always gave us a couple dollars, which we took to Woolworths and spent on bobby pins and paper clips and pens and other things we thought a grown-up might like. Each of us always had a gift to bring, and the older kids helped the younger ones with the wrapping.

My mother never went along to Aunt Nancy's. With us gone she had precious time to be alone with the baby and get ready for Christmas Day. All of us making the trip piled into our big station wagon and my dad drove from our suburb (that was still partly prairie) into the heart of Chicago. Going under viaducts and through tunnels and along crowded, unfamiliar streets was a great adventure and half the fun of the trip.

Aunt Nancy was something of a recluse who lived in a huge residence hotel that had the look and smell of the past century. Most of its residents were elderly people seeking quiet and anonymity. Our family's arrival shattered the quiet. After the inevitable argument over who got to push the elevator button, we rode to the eighth floor and got off in a long hallway lit by wall lamps that cast a pale, yellowish light toward the ceiling. The worn carpet with its faded roses absorbed the sound of our running feet as we raced to the open door where Aunt Nancy awaited us.

Our petite aunt looked like she got stuck in the 1940s. She dressed in Katherine Hepburn-type clothes—all perfectly preserved—and wore bright red lipstick. She dyed her hair and wore it in a curly style that she set in pin curls. I think she wanted to look twenty years old for the rest of her life.

Aunt Nancy's tiny efficiency apartment never changed. She never got new furniture or rearranged what she had. For holiday decoration she set out a little glass Christmas tree. Her treats were always the same too, and made us feel like visiting royalty. There was sure to be a box of assorted cookies nesting in little pleated papers. Each of us got a least one of our favorites. And we each got our very own bottle of Coke—a particular treat in a big family where you always have to share. We also got potato chips, dip, and other treats we never had at home.

Over the years Aunt Nancy worked at various secretarial jobs and didn't make much money at any of them. We were her whole family—as well as her whole Christmas—and she had a genius for choosing the right presents. She also had a genius for receiving them. Unwrapping a card of bobby pins, she went on and on about how she'd just run out of them and how pleased she was that we had thought to get them for her. She made us feel that nobody picked out better presents than we did, even though we probably gave her the same things year after year.

Aunt Nancy's presents to us always suited our ages and interests so well that she must have consulted our mom. I especially remember the year I was five and she gave me a bride doll that was so beautiful I couldn't stop looking at her. Her satiny, lacy dress rustled and crackled at my touch. She wore perfect little shoes and tiny pearl earrings. I named her Betty and stared at her all Christmas Eve.

I also remember the little lion on wheels Aunt Nancy gave to my brother, Pat, and how he took off like a bug down the hallway of the hotel. Then there was the Mighty Matilda Battleship for my brother, Joe. It was a state-of-the-art boy's weapon toy that I desperately wanted for myself.

Of the eight children in our family, all but Teresa had the experience of going to Aunt Nancy's on Christmas Eve. Teresa was a baby the November morning Aunt Nancy boarded the Illinois Central to go to her office job. The train crashed that day, killing forty-four people. Aunt Nancy was one of them.

That year we had a wretched Christmas Eve. All of us got sick to our stomachs, and my dad was very blue. He and Nancy had been especially close. These many years later, he still grieves a little during the Christmas season.

The year Aunt Nancy died, I turned seventeen and left home. It was a major turning point in my life and a very lonesome time for me. As the years have passed—and I look back at my life—the memory of Aunt Nancy is one I cherish. She let few people into her life, and I had the rare and wonderful privilege of being one of them.

Mary Hayes-Grieco

A Sense of Family

We had only been married three months when John was inducted into the service during World War II. He was stationed near Baltimore and I followed. We found one little room in a row house that was two rooms wide and seven or eight rooms deep. Our room was at the very back and terribly cold because everyone was conserving energy. To keep warm at night we spread John's army overcoat on top of the blankets and then piled on other outdoor clothing as well.

Even if John had had a pass, we couldn't have afforded train tickets to visit our families in St. Louis. John's $21 a month paycheck plus the $140 I earned from my civil service job was barely enough to live on.

One Saturday as Christmas approached, we took a bus to the outdoor city market and picked out a small evergreen tree. We stood it on our dresser, and for decorations bought a box of ornaments that were only about an inch in diameter. The thing I remember most about the tree was the string of little American flags we put on it. For many years those flags decorated our Christmas trees, but in time the flags disappeared. We especially wished we still had them the three Christmases our grandson was in the marines, and again during the Gulf War.

On Christmas Day we got together enough money to call St. Louis and talk to both our families. Many years earlier, John's parents had emigrated from Russia, and the family was very close. The entire family gathered at his parents' house to celebrate Christmas. Hearing the clamor and cheer of all those relatives in the background was a reminder of what he was missing: the traditional goose, the homemade pork sausage, the potato pancakes, and his father's expansive holiday toast wishing everyone good health and good fortune and the best of everything the world had to offer.

Since moving to Baltimore we had become friendly with a bedridden mother and her spinster daughters who shared one large bedroom in the row house where we lived. On Christmas Day they invited us for cookies. We had a good laugh about how the daughters kept a bottle of wine under the bed for their mother's health. The nice thing was that John and I were together, and the warmth of friendship we felt with this mother and her daughters gave us the sense of family that is so important at Christmas.

John and Lucille Sukalo

A Simpler and More
Joyful Christmas

When I told friends I was going to be spending Christmas in Man-
agua, they were astounded. This was in 1990, and although
the war in Nicaragua had ended, the country and its people
still suffered greatly. Clearly it was not a place most people
would choose to spend the holidays. I explained the trip by
saying it was my mother's idea, and we would be staying
with the Perrys. They, along with their three children, had
moved from Alabama to Managua and made a three-year
commitment to help the Nicaraguans medically and spiritually.

My mother and I arrived in Managua four days before Christmas. The airport was like something out of the
fifties. Instead of going down a ramp and directly into the
airport, we descended the stairs that had been wheeled up to
the plane. The observation tower was crowded with people
waving and yelling. Although there were no holiday decorations, the atmosphere was festive, which seemed strange because it was so warm. Then I reminded myself that it had
probably been warm in Bethlehem too; the image of coldness
for Christmas was something we invented.

On the way from the airport we stopped at the home
of some missionaries who were hosting a Christmas party.
An ecumenical group of twenty-five or thirty people of all
ages, mostly from the U.S., had gathered. The house was
simple and open with a spacious living area. There were no
Christmas decorations and not much food; the only drink

was water. This was my first clue as to how hard life was in Nicaragua.

The main topic of conversation at the party was a recent presentation of *The Messiah,* which had been televised. Several of the people there had sung in the choir and they engendered compliments and accolades. I couldn't help but think that back home party conversations would be about the crowded malls or holiday preparations or busy social calendars. The highlight of the evening was the singing of Christmas carols. The singing began timidly, but soon the spirit moved through the room, infecting friend and newcomer alike and uniting us in the remembrance of the holiday.

In these first hours in Managua the simplicity brought a real joy to the Christmas season that sang louder and more joyfully than the clarion assault of overabundance at home. The highlights of special programs, carols, and holiday greetings took on meaning more fulfilling and less harrowing than frantic Christmas shopping and extravagant parties. It was, quite simply, freeing.

The Sunday before Christmas we went to a local church. The service was very long and in Spanish, but the music and singing cut through the language barrier. The choir sang familiar as well as local music. A children's choir also sang, and though less talented, they were remarkable. The story of Christmas was alive in their eyes and in the faces of the children who were listening. A precious little girl in a red dress and with an enormous personality held court in the doorway with the sun shining behind her. She deigned who could share her stoop and every now and then she popped into her mother or grandmother's lap. But after a brief stay she would return to her reign with a new friend in tow.

Christmas was sparse in the Perry home. My mother and I brought a lot of candy with us, and on Christmas Eve we stayed up with Alan and Susan to stuff the Ninja Turtle piñata we bought in the market. There weren't a lot of presents, but that only added to the festivity. The Perry children—aged six, eight, and ten—were elated over the simple gifts they received. Here children were thrilled with so little.

Throughout the day there was much coming and going at *Casa Perry*. A Jewish family came by and their children joined in the piñata fun. Later a young Nicaraguan doctor, his wife, and little girl came for dinner. He brought his guitar and he and his wife entertained us with local folk songs and told about life in Nicaragua. Even though his profession put them in the top echelon of society, there was not much hope for them economically. As a resident he made $550 a month, and with massive inflation his salary wasn't enough for them to have a place of their own so they lived with his in-laws. As a doctor he would make only $50 a month more and have to leave his family to live and work on the Atlantic coast. In spite of their hardship, their generosity was overflowing. He had spent an entire day preparing his gift—a wonderful *nocatamale* that he brought to share with everyone.

Christmas in Managua was much simpler than the celebrations I was used to, and it was more joyful. We didn't complain about what we did not have. Instead we were grateful for what we did have and were happy to share it. My time in Managua will always be special because it gave me a new view of Christmas and helped me focus on its true meaning and message.

Adele Stockham

The Gift of Life

After two years of college, I moved to Tucson, Arizona, with my older sister, Carol. Though she had just graduated from college, we both had to work our way up the ladder, surviving on minimum wage jobs. We lived in a one-bedroom apartment with its leaky plumbing and bare concrete floors.

Despite our poverty, I grew to love the constant sunshine, lizards and roadrunners, crimson desert sunsets, and oranges growing on trees instead of on grocery store shelves. Even the prickly cactus began to show me its beauty. I looked forward to the cactus blossoms of spring and a day when I could afford to continue my education.

In early December, Carol and I began thinking about Christmas in our bleak adobe apartment without family and our usual traditions. We dreamed of Norwegian pastries, lefse, Swedish meatballs. Before homesickness set in, Carol's juvenile-onset diabetes threw us into a major crisis. When I came home from work one day, the pain in her eyes told me her condition was serious, though Carol's stubborn "I'll solve it myself" attitude wouldn't let me seek help. It took until 2:00 A.M. for me to convince her to find a doctor. I borrowed the neighbor's car and rushed my sister to the hospital's emergency room. By the time I returned the car and caught the bus for work that morning, Carol was in a coma.

With few friends in Tucson, I was desperately alone and terrified of losing my sister, my best friend. Our parents had always taken care of Carol when she was ill, but we were 2,000 miles apart. I was alone except for daily telephone contact with Mom and Dad. During the next few days,

Carol's blood sugar soared to record setting levels, shocking her new doctors and terrifying my parents and me. And now an added complication: arthritis of the spine.

In her teen and college years Carol had suffered many life-threatening episodes with diabetes. Her will to live and strong faith in God always pulled her through, though this time the doctors' "could be fatal" warning rang in my ears. I wasn't sure how many more times faith could save my sister.

By mid-December I was near panic and called home. "Mom, Dad, I don't think I can handle this alone."

My parents were unable to afford two airline tickets, so Mom came to Tucson by herself. We drew strength from each other and prayed for a miracle. Several days after Mom's arrival, Carol showed signs of improvement. She was no longer comatose, color returned to her face, and her blood sugar lowered dramatically. Hope grew in her smile.

Carol came home that Christmas Eve to our shabby apartment and tiny tree decorated with colored paper chains, strings of popcorn, and borrowed lights. Few gifts lay under the tree, but faith and celebration sparkled in our eyes. Carol was the gift, her health temporarily restored.

I missed Dad and the rest of the family, but I had the greatest gift of all: my sister! For us, home was this strange desert city, its streets lined with glimmering luminaries, Christmas trees made of tumbleweed balls piled in cone shapes, and saguaro cacti adorned with minature lights, their arms pointing to heaven. A desert setting much like that of the first Christmas night in Bethlehem of Judea.

Mary Lee Stevens

Of All the Christmases
Of My Youth

I knew—as my father must have known—who the phone call was about even before my mother said, "It's your dad."

Then my mother was folding clothes into a suitcase and my father was giving orders about chores as though my brother and I had never done them before. Mother pulled Rolland and me out onto the front porch and her breath came in white puffs as she told us where Santa Claus's gifts were hidden in the machine shed. Then my parents were gone, leaving Rolland, seventeen, and me, fifteen, to take care of the farm and make Christmas for our little sisters, Becky and Pammy.

It's so unfair, I told myself out in the barn as I grabbed my milk stool in one hand, the full pail in the other and stepped across the gutter. "Are you going to clean the barn tonight or wait till morning?" I yelled at Rolland. If he cleaned the gutters tonight, I'd have to feed the steers alone. I prayed for a "Tomorrow," but as I passed by him he grunted from between cows, "T'night."

Hours later we crunched through crusted snow to the machine shed and gathered our arms full of wrapped and ribboned packages. The night was perfectly black, perfectly still as we started toward the house. Rolland, just a dark blur ahead of me, stopped under the gnarled branches of the big oak. I stopped too and looked up. Hundreds of stars were frozen in the heavens. Their light, reflected in millions of crystals, made the snow sparkle. The whole earth glowed. We stared for several moments, then, silently, moved on.

Becky and Pammy had been alone in the house while we did chores, so we stomped our feet on the porch to announce our return. Warm air slapped our icy cheeks as we burst into the kitchen. Our sisters were sitting in silence on the couch. Rolland snapped on the radio, and I stirred up some hot cocoa. We took turns in the bathtub. The house swelled with Christmas music, then the salty steam of homemade oyster stew. We played Chinese checkers and Monopoly. We cracked nuts, popped corn, boiled and beat fudge.

Santa came just before bedtime. Both Rolland I heard him, and Becky and Pammy went shrieking out to the front yard. They came back into the house carrying the packages we had so carefully placed on the glowing snow.

The next morning after chores, we loaded our sisters into my mother's car and Rolland drove the sixty-five miles to Grandpa and Grandma's. There we joined our parents, aunts, uncles, and cousins for the Christmas dinner that had been planned at Thanksgiving—the Christmas dinner my grandfather had wanted so badly that he wouldn't let my grandmother tell anyone he was sick. Finally she was so exhausted from caring for him that the neighbor took matters into her own hands and called my parents.

In retrospect, of course, we shouldn't have yielded to Grandpa's wishes and tried to have that last Christmas together. It was too much. Just before noon my father and Uncle Clarence had to call his doctor and the ambulance. Grandpa's heart was failing, his lungs filling. He couldn't breathe. They went with him to the hospital and the rest of us waited for their phone call. Throughout the afternoon, my mother and aunts comforted Grandma as she sat in the bedroom smoothing the blankets and pillows where Grandpa had lain.

Later that day the ambulance had to be called a second time. Grandma had a heart attack at five o'clock. After that Rolland and I left for home with our sisters. We did the chores again that night while my parents were at the hospital.

When I think of all the Christmases of my youth, I remember that one. I don't remember opening gifts myself on Christmas Eve; I don't remember eating Christmas dinner with my cousins; I do remember being afraid for my grandparents. And I remember standing under the stars, the earth aglow around me, and realizing how small I was in the vast universe.

Cheryll K. Ostrom

A Most Precious Book

Frau Tschesche, my German teacher in high school, had recently arrived in the United States and spoke English with a heavy accent. Her shape is best described as rotund, and when some of us developed enough rapport to kid with her, we said that instead of walking she scurried. She wore no makeup, and in a total disregard for style, pulled her hair straight back from her face. Still, there was a beauty about her that lay in her sweet nature and a lovely smile that reflected in her whole face.

Over time, Frau Tschesche revealed a little of her history. During World War II she was a Russian POW. The Russians valued her because of her excellent command of their language and a couple others as well. One story from her life remains vivid to me. It took place at Christmas while she was imprisoned.

Frau Tschesche lived in a dismal barracks with other women prisoners. Over time, they grew very close. As Christmas neared they wanted to exchange gifts, but of course had nothing to give. So they decided to think of imaginary gifts for one another; these were to be presents they would give if it were possible to do so.

While walking through the prison compound a couple days before Christmas, one of the women chanced upon a sprig of greenery from a pine bough. This was a most unusual find because the area around the camp was barren. Perhaps the wind carried the sprig of pine from some distant forest. The woman snatched up the greenery and hid it beneath her coat.

Inside the drab prison barracks stood a single, small stove. On Christmas Eve the women gathered in its circle of warmth. The woman who found the pine sprig brought it with her and slipped it into the fire. Flames licked the sprig, then engulfed and consumed it, filling the air with the aromatic scent of pine. Then the women exchanged their imaginary gifts. Frau Tschesche told our class about only one of the gifts she received that Christmas Eve: a leather-bound book with gold leaf edging the pages. The binding cracked faintly as bindings often do when a book is first opened. The imagined smell of ink and new paper and leather wafted up to her. Words on the ivory-colored pages beckoned her to read.

Although Frau Tschesche said she remembered all her gifts just as clearly, the book was special, something she forever treasured in her memory. I think what she most wanted our German class to glean from her story was an appreciation for the thought these imprisoned women put into choosing gifts for one another. It was, she said, the most unusual and blessed of all her Christmases.

Each year during the holiday season I recall Frau Tschesche's story and know I am richer because she shared it with those of us who were her students.

Kathy Worre

And Then to Sleep

My family lived in a house that had a sun porch off the living room. On the porch was a daybed where I took my naps as a young child. The porch was also where we put our Christmas tree. Because it was cool in the porch area, my mother wrapped me in a feather quilt at nap time.

Before going back to work in the kitchen, Mama plugged in the tree lights. Cozy and blissfully content, I lay inside my quilt cocoon gazing at the glittery balls and the silvery tinsel and dreaming the dreams of a five-year-old. When I squinched my eyes, the lights all went together and the tree became a glowing orb of beauty.

From the kitchen came the clatter of Mama making prune cakes and poppy seed cakes and other delicacies to be enjoyed on Christmas. She sang Polish lullabies as she rolled out the dough. The loving croon of her voice lowered my eyelids as if they were window shades slowly being drawn. Smells of baking mingled with the scent of pine, and sleep waited no longer. As I slipped into my nap, the last sound I heard was a single strand of tinsel dropping onto the linoleum floor.

Marge Buczynski

Our First Christmas

The first Christmas we were married my husband, Bryant, still had a semester of school to finish. We were living in Tuscaloosa and I was a teacher. My salary amounted to $350 per month and that's what we had to live on. Before Christmas I remember shopping and having practically nothing to spend, but we managed to get something for everybody. We bought our mothers each a sewing basket and our grandmothers each a bottle of hand lotion. We wanted to give each other something, too, because I always felt that was important. Bryant needed new shoes, so he bought a pair and we wrapped them up as a gift. There was a new historical novel I wanted, so Bryant bought that for me. Though we didn't have much to spend, we had a wonderful shopping day together.

We were going to spend Christmas with Bryant's parents, but still wanted our own tree. On the block next to us was a very small grocery store and we went there to look at trees. The procedure was to pick out one and take just the tag—not the whole tree—into the store. Bryant did that. Meanwhile, a woman came along who wanted the same tree. She made a ferocious scene about it and the cashier said, "Well, this man has the tag and he has already bought the tree."

At the time I thought this woman was a real witch. (Now I realize she was under all this stress making Christmas dreams come true for her family, and that she was just irritable and at the end of everything. Not enough time, not enough money, and all those things.) Bryant turned to the woman and said, "Here, take the tree. Merry Christmas!"

What my husband did twenty years ago made a great impression on me. Even under pressure he had some insights into what Christmas was all about, and could be very generous. We were not religious at that time. We *enjoyed* not going to church and we slept late on Sunday mornings. But what my husband did that day gave me some insight into his spiritual depth, which was something that I didn't expect or even think of at that very young age. I thought letting the woman have the tree was a beautiful thing for him to do.

That was our first Christmas.

Linda Frye

Prairie Christmas

Long ago, in our Dakota prairie farmhouse, Papa always set up the tree the very afternoon of Christmas Eve. Along with a burst of frosty air and lacy snowflakes, he brought the tree indoors and meticulously shaved the trunk until it fit in the wooden stand. The tree stood in the middle of the frost-covered bay window in the parlor; the tangy scent of pine spreading all through the house heralded a glorious Christmas.

Papa wired in sprigs where growth was sparse and made sure the tree stood straight and tall in the holder that he covered with layers of cotton like low, rolling snowbanks. Then he closed the oak-paneled door leading to the dining room, and no one except Mama was allowed to enter.

Mama and Papa always trimmed the tree. Together they looped ropes of scarlet cranberries and strands of fluffy popcorn around the lush, green boughs. They hung garlands of tinsel too. Some were darkened with age, but each year they added one shiny new length. It began at the top of the star that touched the ceiling, then spiraled down, encircling the tree. Glossy pictures of angels edged in tinsel hung on the boughs, and so did some of Mama's fancier candies made into perfect likenesses of strawberries and cherries complete with stems. These candies weren't for eating; they were just too beautiful. "If you eat them we will miss looking at their loveliness," Mama said.

After the tree was trimmed, we children got to put our surprises under it, but no peeking or poking before we left. Then in and out of the door went Mama, closing it firmly behind her as she rounded up boxes from upstairs and downstairs and even in the cellar. She did her last-minute wrapping with white tissue paper and gummed stickers.

On Christmas Eve we children went upstairs to put on our very best. While I struggled with the buttons on my red velveteen dress, we took turns peeking through the floor register in hopes of glimpsing that wondrous tree, or maybe even Santa. No luck, though. Not ever. All we saw was the coal stove and the orange light shed through the isinglass. All washed, fastened, and inspected, we gathered on the bare, painted steps hardly able to contain our excitement.

After what seemed like forever we heard stomping on the snow-covered front porch and the jingle of sleigh bells. Then Mama called, "Come right away! Santa was just here!" We rushed down the remaining steps to the parlor door. Santa was always gone, of course, but there stood the magnificent tree aglow with the light from wax candles clamped to its branches. When Papa had the last candle lit, we sang "Silent Night." The only light came from the flickering candles on the tree and the glowing coals in the stove.

Right after the singing we rushed into the parlor calling "Merry Christmas everyone!" The presents under the tree were always dreams coming true: a new satin handmade dress for a doll, a bright knit cap, a set of tin doll dishes. With such joy around, everything looked beautiful and glamorous.

Mama played "Holy Night" and "Ave Maria" on the phonograph as we unwrapped gifts. Meanwhile Papa made one last trip outside to where he'd hidden his gift for Mama. He always had a complete surprise for her. The Christmas I remember best he gave her a cut glass sugar bowl and cream pitcher that glistened like jewels in the soft light of the parlor. Mama's face shone with surprise and love. "My, it's so beautiful," she said, "and just what I've always wanted."

What a wonderful blessed Christmas to remember.

Louise Johnson

Fuzzy Blue Slippers
Of Forgiveness

Slippers. There was no need to peek, no need to shake the present from Grandma Grebe. Every blessed year she gave me slippers. When I was a child, she also let me pick a toy from the Spiegel catalog, but even then the slippers were always there.

I never wore slippers. Didn't like slippers. And still Grandma gave me slippers year after year. I was in slipper purgatory—a place of my own making because I had led Grandma to believe that my feet were perpetually cold.

When my brothers and I were little, one of our biggest treats was to spend the weekend at Grandma's small flat. We took turns sleeping with her in the double bed that filled her cubbyhole of a bedroom. The bed fit into the room only one way: squeezed into a corner with a window at its foot.

After putting us to bed, Grandma always stayed up a couple more hours. As an unacknowledged insomniac, I spent the time awake and eventually my mind turned to pranks. I rested my feet on the windowsill until Grandma came to bed. Then when she snuggled in and started her sleep breathing—I don't think she ever admitted how much she snored—I put my icy feet on her legs. Every Christmas she remembered those cold feet with a pair of slippers.

Each year the slippers were a different style: Mickey Mouse slippers, low-cut footies, open-toed slip-ons, ankle-high crocheted booties with pom-poms. Year after year they accumulated under my bed along with the dust bunnies, memorializing Christmases past.

The Christmas I think of now could have been like
any other, the traditions giving a sense of constancy to the
years. The slippers could have been any pair in the slipper
slew. But it wasn't just *any* Christmas. It was our last Christmas with Grandma; these were the last slippers. This was the
Christmas Grandma got mugged.

On Christmas Eve day Grandma went to the grocery
store for our Christmas brunch fixings. In the alley behind
her building, a purse snatcher wrestled her handbag away.
During the struggle, he knocked her down, bruising her face
and dislocating her shoulder. Grandma spent Christmas Eve
in the emergency room, and the rest of the holiday on pain
killers. From time to time she came out of her blur for a
glimpse of the festivities, tugging at a ribbon and, with help,
opening a present only to doze off again.

Grandma was always the center of our Christmas. She
prepared for it all year, adding to her Christmas Club account, finding that special grandchild's gift in July. Her
Christmas decorations were never completely put away, and
her Gene Autry Christmas album always stood ready beneath the hi-fi.

Without her spirit that year of the mugging, the an-
gelic faces of my family tied themselves into an angry knot. It
was as though we saw our own Christmas as a distorted reflection in a shiny tree ornament, an ornament that was now
flawed. There was talk of using the mugger for batting practice, feeding him the contents of the purse, altering his gen-
der.

In Grandma's more lucid moments she shook her
head, her watery blue eyes and strained voice trying to say,
*Don't ruin your Christmas over this; you're hurting yourself; he
must have needed it more than we did.*

My slippers that year were huge, blue fuzzy affairs.
Though I still didn't like slippers, I put that last pair on from
time to time just to feel a little of the warmth that Grandma

154

can no longer share in person. My feet were always colder than I thought and the slippers' warmth would rise up through my feet, shoulders, head and keep going. Long after the slippers had surrendered their fuzz to the dust collection under my bed, they were a reminder of a kind of forgiveness that nearly passes human understanding. Nearly, but not quite.

Coralee Grebe

Grandpa and the
Silver Dollars

---

*I was ten years old when Grandfather Kapplinger died. In my ear-*liest memory of him, I am sitting on his lap listening to him sing lullabies in German. He was a very thin, neat man who smoked a pipe and had about him the aroma of pipe tobacco and the clean smell of soap. When Christmas came, we grandchildren always knew that he was going to give each of us a card in which he enclosed a silver dollar.

A lot of elderly men want to sit back and let some-body take care of them. But not Grandpa, and especially not at Christmas. Until his death at eighty-seven, he chose his own cards and wrote personal notes on each one. On mine he always wrote, "My dear Dana . . ." and then said something about having a Merry Christmas and a wonderful year. Of course along with the card there was that prized silver dollar.

Some of my cousins saved their silver dollars and still had them years later. For certain I didn't save mine, and I have no recollection of how any of them were spent except for the last one Grandpa gave me. After he died, my mother asked the four of us kids to give her our silver dollars. She used them to buy Bibles that cost ninety-nine cents apiece, and gave one to each of us.

That Bible was the best investment my mother could have made. Although more than forty years have passed since then, this plain little King James Version—with every-thing Jesus said printed in red—has always been my favorite Bible. It is the one I read from cover to cover and the one I took for my confirmation. It is the one that I underlined and wrote on in the margins. It is the one that is now ratty and falling apart, yet it is still the Bible I always reach for. I just wish that somewhere inside the front cover it was signed, "My dear Dana with love from your Grandpa Kapplinger."

Dana Jacobson

Christmas at Grandma's

I was an only child until I was six years old and life was wonderful, especially at Christmas. My dad loved the holidays and always decorated the house. I helped him decorate the tree, and he told me about Santa, and I loved everything about Christmas. Besides being an only child, I was the first grandchild and my grandparents adored me.

Then my sister was born on December 16 and my world changed overnight. Mother had a difficult birth and developed a severe infection. She had to stay in the hospital through the holidays and for several weeks afterward.

Just before Christmas, my dad lost his job. At the time the country was in the middle of the Depression. My mother was very ill and my dad was worried sick—as were my grandparents—but I was taken to stay with them anyway. Amidst all of the trauma, nobody remembered Christmas. There was no tree, we had no decorations, and Santa never did show up.

Santa came the next year, of course, but by that time I was seven and no longer believed in him. There have been many wonderful Christmases in my life since then, but after all these years I am still vaguely worried and anxious when Christmas approaches. I will never forget that year when Santa could not find me at Grandma's.

Dorothy McGlauchlin

What If There Were No Christmas?

One year when I was working for VISTA (Volunteers in Service to America), someone was needed to play Santa for the retarded adults who worked at the day activity center. My co-workers held a contest, and I think I was finally chosen because of the round, metal-frame glasses I sometimes wore. Everyone understood that I wasn't selected because they thought I shared a lot of traits with the jolly, generous Saint Nick; they just hoped that playing him might make me act a little more Christmasy.

The people for whom I would be playing Santa worked in the activity center and lived in a halfway house for the mildy retarded. Those who developed adequate skills left the group home and lived independently. Those whose condition worsened went to a more institutionalized setting. Because my girlfriend at the time worked in the halfway house, I knew some of the people who lived there and worked at the center.

The party at the activity center was scheduled for noon a couple days before Christmas. I got dressed in my Santa suit and picked up the bag of small, wrapped gifts I was supposed to give out. As I walked in the door of the center, I tried to adopt the hearty Ho Ho Ho persona of the character. But right away I had the sinking feeling I wasn't doing too well. A fellow about nineteen came up and scoffed, "You're not Santa Claus." Then apparently having second thoughts, he moved in close. Putting his face a couple inches from mine, he asked, ". . . are you?"

"Well I certainly am," I said. He seemed satisfied.

A little later this same young man told me he was going to commit suicide. Naturally I was taken aback and wondered if any Santa had ever come up against such a situation. It occurred to me to say, "Why don't you wait until you open your gift?" but instead I murmured something kind of lame, like, "Maybe you shouldn't do that."

A woman in her fifties with a shuffling gait and the undisguised curiosity of a child came up to me. Her name was Mary. I knew her, but dressed as I was, she didn't recognize me. We looked into each other's eyes, and it was clear she never for a moment doubted that I was Santa Claus. Then with utter sincerity and simplicity she began singing to me. Since that day I have often tried to recall the song she sang, but I cannot. Maybe that's because it's really not important. What made the song so memorable was the way Mary sang it. Standing before me in the body of a fifty-year-old was a child whose voice rang with sweetness and poignancy because she believed she was singing to Santa.

The incident has remained vivid in my memory because Mary reminded me that in our culture Christmas is about belief. Children believe in Santa Claus and his ability to grant their wishes. Adults have Christ and the belief that by following his teachings they will be fulfilled in this life and rewarded in the next.

About ten years ago I became quite cynical about Christmas, and especially about the commercialization of the whole holiday season. But then I began thinking, *What if there were no Christmas? What if we never had a special time to think about the place that peace, love, and goodwill have in our lives?*

Whenever I start feeling humbug about the holidays, I remember Mary and that look of belief in her eyes. It's always enough to make me start believing in Christmas again.

Lee Henschel, Jr.